how2become

A Railway
Signaller

THE INSIDER'S GUIDE

Orders: Please contact How2become Ltd, Suite 2, 50 Churchill Square Business Centre, Kings Hill, Kent ME19 4YU. You can also order via the e mail address info@how2become.co.uk.

ISBN: 9781910202302

First published 2014

Typeset for How2become Ltd by Gnibel.com.

Printed in Great Britain for How2become Ltd by:
CMP (uk) Limited, Poole, Dorset.

CONTENTS

INTRODUCTION

Dear Sir/Madam,

Welcome to **how2become a Railway Signaller: The Insider's Guide.** This guide has been designed to help you prepare for and pass the Railway Signaller selection process. We feel certain that you will find the guide both a comprehensive and highly informative tool for helping you obtain a career that is highly sought after.

The Railway Signaller selection process is not easy to pass. Many people apply to become a signaller as they want to gain experience working for a Train Operating Company before progressing to the role of train driver. You must prepare fully if you are to pass the selection process and be offered a position as a Railway Signaller. There are a number of things that you can do in order to increase your chances of success, and they are all contained within this guide. The majority of Train Operating Companies (TOCs) are both professional and meticulous in how they run their assessment centres and you should find the process an enjoyable one. We hope that you enjoy the guide and we wish you all the best in your pursuit of becoming a signaller.

If you would like any further assistance with the selection process then we offer many other products and training courses via our website www.how2become.com. Finally, you won't achieve much in life without hard work, determination and perseverance. Work hard, stay focused and be what you want!

Good luck and best wishes,

The how2become team

The How2become Team

PREFACE BY AUTHOR RICHARD McMUNN

Before I get into the guide and teach you how to prepare for the selection process, it is important that I explain a little bit about my background and why I am qualified to help you succeed.

I joined the Royal Navy soon after leaving school and spent four fabulous years in the Fleet Air Arm branch on-board HMS Invincible. It had always been my dream to become a Firefighter and I only ever intended staying the Royal Navy for the minimum amount of time. At the age of 21 I left the Royal Navy and joined Kent Fire and Rescue Service. Over the next 17 years I had an amazing career with a fantastic organisation. During that time I was heavily involved in training and recruitment, often sitting on interview panels and marking application forms for those people who wanted to become Firefighters. I also worked very hard and rose to the rank of Station Manager. I passed numerous assessment centres during my time in the job and I estimate that I was successful at over 95% of interviews I attended.

The reason for my success was not because I am special in anyway, or that I have lots of educational qualifications,

because I don't! In the build-up to every job application or promotion I always prepared myself thoroughly. I found a formula that worked and that is what I intend to teach you throughout the duration of this book.

Over the past few years I have taught many people how to pass the selection process for becoming signallers, train conductors and also trainee train drivers. As you are probably aware, many people want to become signallers. In fact, Network Rail trains approximately 400-500 new signallers every year. As a result of this, the competition can be quite fierce. However, the vast majority of people who do apply will submit poor application forms or they will do very little to prepare for the assessment centre and the interview. As a result, they will fail.

The way to pass the selection process is to embark on a comprehensive period of intense preparation. I would urge you to use an action plan during your preparation. This will allow you to focus your mind on exactly what you need to do in order to pass. For example, if it has been many years since you last attended an interview, then you will probably have a lot of work to do in this area. If it has been many years since you last sat a test, then you may have to work very hard in order to pass the psychometric tests that form part of the assessment centre. The point I am making here, is that it is within your power to improve on your weak areas. If you use an action plan then you are far more likely to achieve your goals.

I use action plans in just about every element of my work. Action plans work simply because they focus your mind on what needs to be done. Once you have created your action plan, stick it in a prominent position such as your fridge door. This will act as a reminder of the work that you need to do in order to prepare properly for selection. Your action plan might look something like this:

MY WEEKLY ACTION PLAN FOR PREPARING FOR RAILWAY SIGNALLER SELECTION

Monday	Tuesday	Wednesday	Thursday	Friday
Research into the TOC I am applying for. Includes reading recruitment literature and visiting websites.	60 minute Interview preparation including preparing my responses to questions.	Obtain application form and read recruitment literature and application form guidance notes.	Research into the TOC I am applying for. Includes reading recruitment literature and visiting websites.	60 minute mock interview with a friend or relative.
60 minutes preparation on psychometric tests, including Observational Ability Test.	30 minute Checking Tests preparation.	45 minute reading up on the role of a railway signaller and the job description/ person specification.	60 minutes preparation on psychometric tests, including Observational Ability Test.	30 minute Assessing Information Test preparation.
20 minute jog or brisk walk.	30 minutes gym work.	REST PERIOD – no fitness or exercise.	20 minute jog or brisk walk.	30 minutes gym work.

Note: Saturday and Sunday, rest days.

The above sample action plan is just a simple example of what you may wish to include. Your action plan will very much depend on your strengths and weaknesses. After reading this guide, decide which areas you need to work on and then add them to your action plan. Areas that you may wish to include in your action plan could be:

- Researching the role of a railway signaller;

- Researching the training that you will undergo as a siganller and the necessary requirements of the role;

- Researching the Train Operating Company that you are applying for;

- Dedicating time to completing the application form and reading the guidance notes;

- Carrying out practice tests that are similar to the ones required at the assessment centre, such as the Observational Ability Test;

- Light fitness work in order to keep up your concentration levels and improve your positive state of mind;

- Interview preparation including carrying out a mock interview.

You will note that throughout the duration of this guide I make continued reference to 'preparation'. During my career I have been successful at over 95% of interviews and assessments that I've attended. The reason for this is simply because I always embark on a period of focused preparation, and I always aim to improve on my weak areas. Follow this simple process and you too can enjoy the same levels of success that I have enjoyed.

Finally, it is very important that you believe in your own abilities. It does not matter if you have no qualifications. It does not matter if you have no knowledge yet of the role of a Railway Signaller. What does matter is self-belief, self-discipline and a genuine desire to improve and become successful.

Enjoy reading the guide and then set out on a period of intense preparation!

Best wishes,

Richard McMunn

Richard McMunn

DISCLAIMER

Every effort has been made to ensure that the information contained within this guide is accurate at the time of publication. How2become Ltd is not responsible for anyone failing any part of any selection process as a result of the information contained within this guide. How2become Ltd and their authors cannot accept any responsibility for any errors or omissions within this guide, however caused. No responsibility for loss or damage occasioned by any person acting, or refraining from action, as a result of the material in this publication can be accepted by How2become Ltd.

The information within this guide does not represent the views of any third party service or organisation.

CHAPTER ONE

THE ROLE OF A RAILWAY SIGNALLER

In very basic terms, signallers operate the signals and points that help ensure the trains run safely and on time. It is a safety-critical role and you must be capable of working, unsupervised whilst following strict procedural and safety guidelines. You will need to maintain high safety standards during both normal rail running procedures and also when there are incidents and disruption on the track. Disruption usually occurs when there are trespassers on a track or, more often than not, when a train is running late. Working as a signaller requires outstanding communication skills, a strong sense of responsibility, an ability to work under pressure and the ability to make systematic decisions in a timely fashion.

Railway signallers usually work as part of a team that manages operational safety and train services for a specific geographical location. The Train Operating Companies who employ signallers place enormous emphasis on responsibility

for the safety of their passengers, their colleagues and their stakeholders/partners. In order to become a signaller you must be calm, methodical and analytical, so you can make all your decisions accurately after proper consideration.

As well as good hearing, eyesight and normal colour perception you'll need good concentration skills too. There will be times when you need to maintain your attention even when there is not much happening and other times when you need to focus on the detail to make sure an activity is performed correctly or switch between many different activities, for example when train services are disrupted.

You must be able to assess situations and think through the outcome of your actions under pressure. In many cases you'll be the only one in your signal box, so self-motivation and the ability to work alone are essential.

THE SKILLS AND QUALITIES REQUIRED FOR THE ROLE OF A RAILWAY SIGNALLER

Whilst not exhaustive, the following list will give you a good idea of the types of skills, qualities and attributes required to perform the role competently. I recommend you take note of these as you will need to demonstrate each and every one of them throughout the selection process.

- Excellent awareness of safety (being safety conscious)
- Outstanding communication skills
- Capable of concentrating for long periods of time
- Able to work alone, often unsupervised
- Willing to learn and retain large amounts of job-specific information

- Can work as part of a team

- Mentally and physically fit

- In good health

- Effective listening skills

- Able to interpret written and oral communication

- Flexible and a willingness to work unsociable hours

- Customer-focused

- Able to remain calm and work under pressure

The following is a good example of a typical Railway Signaller job description:

EXAMPLE RAILWAY SIGNALLER JOB DESCRIPTION

Your decisions make all the difference. Taking the lead on signalling during your shift, you'll take great care to make sure trains travel safely and efficiently along the network. You'll keep Britain moving.

About the role
As a guardian of safety and good communications on the railway, you'll ensure the safe passage of trains. Maintaining the highest standards in every action you take, you'll make sure each decision is thought through, following clear, calm and methodical analysis. Even under pressure, your standards will never slip.

You'll work on a shift basis. As the focal point of railway operations in your assigned area, you'll be expected to take the lead in your duties during your shift. That means you'll take command of situations, with an assertive approach and clear communication.

If you pass our assessment, you'll be required to undertake a 9-week residential course at a state-of-the-art training centre. This will be followed by further training within your appointed signal box. We'll make sure you have all the knowledge and skills you need to succeed.

To join us, you'll need to demonstrate:

- The ability to concentrate for long periods
- A calm, methodical and precise approach to your work
- Excellent communication skills
- Good hearing and eyesight, with normal colour perception
- Your own transport, so you can reach your base day and night
- We'll expect you to be:
    - Able to assess situations and consider the impact of your decisions
    - Highly conscientious
    - Willing and able to work shifts, including evenings and weekends

Now that we understand a little bit more about the role of a Railway Signaller, let's now take a look at the all-important recruitment process.

THE RECRUITMENT PROCESS

APPLICATION FORM

This is the first stage of the selection process and one of the toughest to get stages to get through, simply because there will be so many people applying for the posts available. Having said that, I can confidently state that the vast majority of people applying will be very poorly prepared and their form will not get through. Whilst I will go in to greater details later on about the application form, it will generally consist of the following sections:

- General personal details

- Employment history

- Education and qualifications

- References

- Personal development

- Reasons for applying

- Experience of specific work-related situations

- Motivation

- Equal opportunities

- CV upload

- Drugs and alcohol statement

- Declaration

Many of the sections on the application form are relatively easy to complete/pass; however, some of the sections such as reasons for applying and experience of specific work-related situations require you to provide EVIDENCE of where you have previously demonstrated a particular quality, such as safety, communication, customer service and concentration. Later on within this guide I will teach you exactly how to answer these questions correctly.

Network Rail will normally require you to apply and submit your application or the role online, so it is important that you have access to a computer and internet access.

On receipt of the application form you will be sent a situational judgement assessment (SJT). The application and the situational judgement assessment are pre-screening tools which allow Network Rail to check that you are a good fit for the position of signaller and provide an initial filter on applicants.

THE ASSESSMENT CENTRE
If you are invited to attend an Assessment Centre at one of Network Rails

Centres, there will be a number of assessments that you will be asked to undertake. The tests will usually comprise of assessments that will test a particular set of skills. The tests will be of similar format to the following tests that we have designed to ensure you are prepared:

Checking Tests
This assessment measures your ability to find a fault in a sequence of operating buttons and provides useful information about your planning and decision making skills.

Observational Ability Test
This is an assessment designed to assess some specific aspects of your attention skills including how well you can

divide your attention and how well you can sustain attention over a period of time.

Assessing Information Tests
This assessment is designed to look at your ability to understand comprehension and assess the information you are given regarding a particular scenario.

INTERVIEW
If you are successful at the Assessment Centre stage, you will be invited to attend an interview. This will take place with the Line Manager and will involve a variety of questions. All candidates will be asked questions that are designed to assess your capabilities in the 8 core non-technical skills areas. Specifically they will assess how you respond to particular scenarios and your preferences for different ways of working. The 8 core non-technical skills are as follows:

Conscientiousness – the ability to work diligently, with a positive attitude and be willing to take responsibility for their own actions.

Relationships with People – the ability to work with others in the team in a positive, respectful and supportive manner; providing support and help when needed and managing conflict when required.

Communications – the ability to communicate both verbally and in written format clearly and concisely and to stand your ground as necessary.

Willingness and Ability to Learn – the ability and motivation to be trained, retain information, apply it in the work environment and learn and develop on the job.

Planning and Decision Making – the ability to anticipate, plan and prioritise activities.

Multi Task Capacity – the ability to successfully carry out more than one task at a time.

Controlled Under Pressure – the ability to cope in emergency or degraded situations.

Attention Management – the ability to remain alert and focussed, to manage distractions, and keep an awareness of the overall situation.

At the end of the interview the manager also makes an assessment of your speaking and listening skills. This includes things like how well you have spoken and been able to phrase your answers to the questions; how you have organised the information you are providing and how you listen and show you are listening.

HOW AND WHERE TO APPLY

I would recommend you apply for Railway Signalling jobs directly through the Network rail website at the following link:

www.networkrail.co.uk

CHAPTER TWO
MY 7 TOP INSIDER TIPS
AND ADVICE FOR SUCCESS

TIP 1 – BE PATIENT, PERSISTENT AND ALWAYS LOOK FOR WAYS TO IMPROVE ON YOUR WEAK AREAS

Many popular jobs, including the job of a Railway Signaller, are difficult to obtain. There are a number of reasons for this but the main one is the competition. Many people will apply for the position of signaller when advertised, so you need to stand out from the crowd in order to progress through each stage. Ask yourself how serious you are about becoming a Railway Signaller? Are you prepared to keep trying if you fail at one of the stages? Are you prepared to work hard to improve yourself and take the time required to prepare for the selection process?

The main thing to remember is that you can achieve your goal, providing you are prepared to work hard and improve.

There are many ways of improving your chances of success and this guide will help you to understand them. I would strongly advise that you utilise an action plan to help you to concentrate on your weak areas. Whilst I have already covered this during the early stage of the guide, it is worth mentioning it again. Within your action plan try to include lots of focus on your weak areas. Let's say for example you are not confident at your ability to pass the Observational Ability Test, which is a similar test to that of the real assessment. Within your action plan you will need to write down exactly what you plan to do in order to improve in this weak area – then take action. This may include:

- Carrying out 20 minutes worth of timed tests five nights per week that will help to improve your scores at the assessment centre.

- Obtaining further practice booklets with sample test questions. I recommend Observational Ability testing tool which is available through Amazon.co.uk or How2become.com.

- Employing the services of a personal tutor, if required.

The key to improvement is to carry out what I call 'deliberate and repetitive' practice. This effectively means finding out exactly what you are weak at, and then carrying out lots of targeted practice until you can do it with your eyes closed! Not literally, but hopefully you get my point.

TIP 2 – LEARN ABOUT THE COMPANY YOU ARE APPLYING FOR

Put yourself in the shoes of the recruitment officer at Network Rail, or the organisation you are applying to join as a Signaller. What type of person do you want to employ? The answer

should be obvious – you would want to employ someone who has researched both the role and organisation, in-depth.

When you complete the application form you will have the opportunity to make reference to the reasons why you want to become a Railway Signaller. Throughout this guide I will show you how to increase your chances of success and demonstrate that you are serious about joining Network Rail or the organisation you have applied to.

TIP 3 – PRACTISE PLENTY OF TEST QUESTIONS

You'd be surprised at how many candidates attend the assessment centre having carried out little or no preparation whatsoever. Don't be one of those people who are ill-prepared.

The selection process involves a number of different tests. We have provided you with tests that will assess similar qualities to that of your real test. Types of assessments that you should practice include:

- Assessing Information Tests
- Checking Tests
- Observational Ability Tests (OAT)
- Situational Judgement Tests (SJT)

There are a number of ways that you can increase your chances of success and within this guide I will show you how.

In addition to practising the sample tests that I have provided within this guide, I strongly encourage you to obtain additional testing books and resources. Just by practising different psychometric tests your brain will begin to work quicker and more effectively and it is important that you take the time to

do this. Make sure you allocate plenty of time in your action plan to each of the testing areas indicated above.

TIP 4 – DEMONSTRATE AN AWARENESS OF SAFETY

Being safe and having the ability to follow safety rules and regulations is crucial to the role. Safety must always come first! As a fully qualified Railway Signaller you have a lot of responsibility in relation to safety rules and procedures. If you cannot follow these rules and procedures, then you will not make a competent Signaller.

Throughout the selection process you will be assessed against this important area and it is essential that you have it at the forefront of your mind at all times. When completing the application form you may be asked to provide an example of where you have been responsible for safety, or where safety has played an important part in a group or individual task. Think about your responses carefully and include answers that demonstrate your knowledge and understanding of the importance of safety. If you have any experience of carrying out a safety conscious role during current or previous employment then I would advise that you include this in your application form responses.

To learn more about safety in the workplace take a look at the Government's own Health and Safety website. This can be found at the following web address: www.hse.gov.uk

TIP 6 – BE SMART AND PRESENTABLE

It goes without saying, but you'd be amazed at how many people turn up to the assessment centre, and even the interview, in jeans and a t-shirt! Unsurprisingly, this does not go down well with the recruitment staff.

You are applying for a highly sought after post with an organisation that sets itself high standards. Therefore, it is important that you set yourself high standards right from the offset. Whenever you come into contact with the recruitment staff, you should always ensure that you are wearing formal clothing in the form of shirt and tie for men or smart dress for women. Make sure you are clean shaven and that your shoes are clean and tidy. You only get one chance to make a first impression, so make sure it's a positive one.

Another piece of important advice is not to be late for any of your appointments. It is far better to arrive 15 minutes early than 1 minute late. There is a big emphasis by Network Rail and the Train Operating Companies on ensuring the trains run on time. Therefore, they want to employ Railway Signallers who are capable of getting to work on time.

TIP 7 – NEWTWORK RAIL FIRST, RAILWAY SIGNALLER SECOND

As you can imagine, many applicants are not too bothered about working for Network Rail, so long as they get to become a Railway Signaller! In my view, this is a mistake and it will not assist them in their application. Throughout the application process you should demonstrate that you have a desire to join Network Rail, as opposed to being hell bent on simply becoming a Signaller. The way to achieve this is to learn just as much about the organisation you are applying for as you do about the role of a Signaller. During the interview there is a strong possibility that you will be asked questions similar to the following:

Q. Why do you want to work for our company?

Q. What research have you carried out into our company?

Q. What significant events have happened in this industry over the past 12 months?

Q. What has attracted you to our company?

During your preparation for becoming a Railway Signaller make sure you carry out plenty of research into the organisation you are applying for.

CHAPTER THREE
HOW TO CREATE AN EFFECTIVE CV

As I discussed earlier in the guide, you may be required to upload your CV when you apply to become a Railway Signaller. During this section of the guide I will provide you with a step-by-step guide on how to create a CV that is both effective and relevant to the job you are applying for.

The word Curriculum Vitae translated means the 'course of life'. CV's are used to demonstrate to an employer that you have the potential, the skills, and the experience to carry out the role you are applying for. Your CV is a very important document and you should spend sufficient time designing it so that it matches the job that you are applying for as closely as possible.

WHAT MAKES AN EFFECTIVE CV?

In simple terms an effective CV is one that matches the specification and the requirements of the job you are applying

for. Your CV should be used as a tool to assist you in your application for becoming a Railway Signaller and it should be centred on the following areas:

- Creating the right impression of yourself;
- Indicating that you possess the right qualities and attributes to perform the role;
- Grabbing the organisation's (Network Rail) attention;
- Being concise and clear.

The most effective CV's are the ones that make the assessor's job easy. They are simple to read, to the point, relevant and focus on the job/role that you are applying for. CV's should not be overly long unless an employer specifically asks for this. Effective CV writing is an acquired skill that can be obtained relatively quickly with a little bit of time, effort and focus.

Before you begin to start work on your CV it is a good idea to have a basic idea of how a job/person specification is constructed. A job description/person specification is basically a blueprint for the role you are applying for; it sets out what the employer expects from potential applicants. One of your main focus points during the construction of your CV will be to match the job/person specification of the Railway Signaller. Most job/person specifications will include the following areas:

EXPERIENCE REQUIRED: previous jobs, unpaid work experience, life experience, skills, knowledge and abilities: for example, languages, driving, knowledge of specialist fields, ability to use equipment, plus some indication of the level of competence required, and whether the person must have the skills or knowledge beforehand or can learn them on the job.

QUALIFICATIONS REQUIRED: exams, certificates, degrees, diplomas (some jobs require specific qualifications, but most do not and it can be fairer to ask for the skills or knowledge represented by the qualification rather than asking for the qualification itself).

PERSONAL ATTRIBUTES REQUIRED: such as ability to concentrate, a willingness to work on one's own and the ability to work within a team environment.

PERSONAL CIRCUMSTANCES: such as residing in a certain area and being able to work weekends or evenings.

Most job/person specifications will be based around a task analysis of the vacancy, so there should be nothing within the job description/person specification that is irrelevant or that does not concern the particular role you are applying for. Whatever requirements you are asked to meet, you should try hard to match them as closely as possible, providing evidence if possible of your previous experience.

WHAT ARE NETWORK RAIL LOOKING FOR IN YOUR CV?

As previously stated you should ensure that you make the assessor's job as simple as possible. Try to put yourself in the shoes of the assessor. How would you want an applicant's CV to look? You would want it to be relevant to role they are applying for and you would want it to be neat, concise and well organised. You need to spend some time thinking about the type of person the organization you are applying to work with are looking for and how you can match the specification that is relevant to the job you want. Most job specifications will list the essential/desirable requirements in terms of education, qualifications, training, experience, skills, personality and any other special requirements.

Let's take a look at some of the skills required to become a Railway Signaller.

EXAMPLE RAILWAY SIGNALLER JOB DESCRIPTION

Your decisions make all the difference. Taking the lead on signalling during your shift, you'll take great care to make sure trains travel safely and efficiently along the network. You'll keep Britain moving.

About the role

As a guardian of safety and good communications on the railway, you'll ensure the safe passage of trains. Being self-disciplined and maintaining the highest standards in every action you take, you'll make sure each decision is thought through, following clear, calm and methodical analysis. Even under pressure, your standards will never slip.

You'll work on a shift basis. As the focal point of railway operations in your assigned area, you'll be expected to take the lead in your duties during your shift. That means you'll take command of situations, with an assertive approach and clear communication.

If you pass our assessment, you'll be required to undertake a 9-week residential course at a state-of-the-art training centre. This will be followed by further training within your appointed signal box. We'll make sure you have all the knowledge and skills you need to succeed.

To join us, you'll need to demonstrate:

- The ability to concentrate for long periods and follow rules/procedures
- A calm, methodical and precise approach to your work
- Excellent communication skills
- Good hearing and eyesight, with normal colour perception
- Your own transport, so you can reach your base day and night

We'll expect you to be:

- Able to assess situations and consider the impact of your decisions
- Highly conscientious and a knowledge of Rail Regulations
- Willing and able to work shifts, including evenings and weekends

You will see from the above details that some of the key elements of the role include an ability to follow rules and procedures, a level of self-discipline, being calm and knowledge of rail regulations. Once you have the above information then you will be able to mold your CV around the key aspects of the job.

Before I provide you with a sample CV that is based on matching the above role, let's first of all take a look at some of the key elements of a CV.

THE KEY ELEMENTS OF A CV

The following is a list of information I recommend you include within your Railway Signaller CV. Try to put them in this order and remember to be brief and to the point. Make sure you include and highlight the positive aspects of your experience and achievements.

- Your personal details

- Your profile

- Your employment history

- Your academic acievements

- Your interests

- Any other information

- Your references

Let's now take a look at each of the above sections and what you need to include.

YOUR PERSONAL DETAILS

When completing this section you should include the following details:

- Your full name

- Address

- Date of birth

- Nationality

- Contact telephone numbers including home and mobile

- E-mail address

PROFILE

To begin with try to write a brief but to the point statement about yourself making sure you include the keywords that best describe your character. Some effective words to use when describing you, might include:

> *Ambitious, enthusiastic, safety-conscious, customer-focused, ability to concentrate, work unsupervised, calm under pressure, motivated, flexible, caring, trustworthy, meticulous, sense of humour, drive, character, determination, will to succeed, passionate, loyal, team worker, hard-working etc.*

The above words are all powerful and positive aspects of an individual's character. Try to think of your own character and what positive words you can use that best describe you.

Within your profile description try to include a statement that is relative to you and that will make Network Rail think you are the right person for the job, such as:

"I am an extremely conscientious and hard working person who has a great deal of experience in safety-critical situations. I have very good organisational and motivational skills and I am always striving to improve myself. I believe that I would embrace the challenges that this new role has to offer and I am able to learn large amounts of job relevant information and procedures."

EMPLOYMENT HISTORY

When completing this section try to ensure that it is completed in reverse chronological order. Provide the reader with dates, locations and employers, and remember to include your job title. Give a brief description of your main achievements and try to include words of a positive nature, such as:

Achieved, developed, progressed, managed, created, succeeded, devised, drove, expanded, directed.

It is also a good idea to quantify your main achievements, such as:

"During my time with this employer I was responsible for carrying out difficult tasks whilst under pressure and making timely decisions."

ACADEMIC ACHIEVEMENTS

When completing this section include the dates, names and locations of the schools, colleges or universities that you attended in chronological order.

You should also include your qualifications and any other relevant achievements such as health and safety qualifications, customer service courses and/or first aid qualifications. Anything that is relevant to the role you're applying for would be an advantage.

INTERESTS

Within this section try to include interests that match the requirements of the job and ones that also portray you in a positive manner. Maybe you have worked within the voluntary sector or have even carried out some charity work in the past? If so, try to include these in your CV as they show you have a caring and concerning nature. In relation to the role of a Railway Signaller, the following activities and past times are recommended:

- Playing a team sport or activity. This demonstrates you have the ability to work with others as part of a team and concentrate.

- Recent study activities such as learning a new qualification. This demonstrates that you are able to learn and retain a large amount of job specific information.

- Playing a musical instrument. This demonstrates you have the ability to learn new something new and that you also have the patience and determination to succeed and also an ability to concentrate.

OTHER INFORMATION

Within this section of your CV you can include any other information that is relevant to your skills or experiences that you may feel are of benefit. Examples of these could be certificates of achievement from school or work.

REFERENCES

Within this section try to include your current or previous employer, providing you know that they are going to write positive things about you. Be careful who you choose as a reference and make sure you seek their permission first prior to putting down their name and contact details. It may also be a good idea to ask them if you can have a copy of what they have written about you for reference later.

SAMPLE CV

The following sample CV has been designed to give you an idea of how an effective CV might look. It has been created with the position of Railway Signaller in mind. All of the information provided is fictitious.

CURRICULUM VITAE OF RICHARD McMUNN

Address: 11, Any Street, Anytown, Anyshire. ANY 111
Date of birth: 11/01/1971
Nationality: British
Telephone: 01227 XXXXX / Mobile 07890 XXX XXX
E-Mail: richardmcmunn@anyemailaddress.co.uk

PERSONAL PROFILE OF RICHARD MCMUNN

I am an extremely fit and active person who has a great passion for the Rail industry and I have a track record of high-achievement. I have very good organisational, motivational and safety-critical skills and I am always striving to improve myself. I believe that I would embrace the challenges that this new role has to offer. I am a motivated, dedicated, loyal, flexible, conscientious and ambitious person who has the ability to work both within a team and also unsupervised.

I already have a large amount of experience in the working environment and take on a large number of responsibilities both at work, around the home and in my leisure time activities. I currently hold a Health and Safety qualification and I am fully aware of the importance of safety in the role that I am applying for. I have experience in working in pressurised situations where an ability to make timely decisions is crucial.

I also have the ability to act as a role model for the organisation I am working for. I understand that the role of a Railway Signaller does not just involve operating signals and switches, but it also means reacting to ever-changing situations and making safe, decisive decisions in a timely fashion to ensure the trains operate on time.

To conclude, I am a fit, motivated, active, organised and professional individual who has a lot of skills and experiences to offer Network Rail.

EMPLOYMENT HISTORY OF RICHARD MCMUNN (IN CHRONOLOGICAL ORDER)

Job position/title/company #1 goes here   Date of employment goes here

During my time with this employer I was responsible for motivating my team and organising different activities.

Job position/title/company #2 goes here   Date of employment goes here

During my time with this employer I was responsible stock taking and dealing with customer's queries and complaints. I also took on the responsibility of arranging the company's annual staff leisure activity event which often included some form of motivational talk.

Job position/title/company #3 goes here

Date of employment goes here

During my time with this employer I undertook a training course in health and safety and first aid. Part of my role included managing resources and carrying out risk assessments as and when required.

ACADEMIC ACHIEVEMENTS OF RICHARD MCMUNN

Health and Safety qualification   Date of achievement goes here

First Aid qualification   Date of achievement goes here

GSCE Maths Grade C   Date of achievement goes here

GCSE English Grade C   Date of achievement goes here

GCSE Physical Education
Grade B   Date of achievement goes here

INTERESTS AND HOBBIES OF RICHARD MCMUNN

I am an extremely fit and active person who carries out a structured training programme at my local gym five times a week. During my training sessions I will carry out a variety of different exercises such as indoor rowing, cycling, treadmill work and light weights. I measure my fitness levels by performing the multi-stage fitness test once a week and I can currently achieve level 14.5. In addition to my gym work I am a keen swimmer and

break up my gym sessions with long swim sessions twice a week. I can swim 60 lengths of my local swimming pool in time of 35 minutes. I am also the Captain of my local football team and play in the position of midfield. I am also responsible for organising and arranging the weekly training sessions.

In addition to my sporting activities I like to relax with a weekly Yoga group at my local community centre. I also have a keen interest in art and attend evening classes during the months October through to December.

FURTHER INFORMATION

Six months ago I decided to carry out a sponsored fitness event in order to raise money for a local charity. I swam 60 lengths of my local swimming pool, and then ran 26 miles before cycling 110 miles all in one day. In total I managed to raise over £10,000 for charity.

REFERENCES

Name, address and contact details of reference #1

Name, address and contact details of reference #2

TOP TIPS FOR CREATING AN EFFECTIVE CV

New application = new CV

It is important that every time you apply for a job you re-evaluate the content of your CV so that you can match the skills and qualifications required. As a rule you should complete a new CV for every job application unless your applications are close together and the job/person specification is relatively the same. Don't become complacent or allow your CV to get out of date.

Don't pad out your CV

There is a common misconception amongst many job applicants that you need to make your CV scores of pages long for it to get recognised. This simply isn't true. When creating your CV aim for quality rather than quantity. If I was looking through an applicant's CV then I would much prefer to see three to five pages of high quality focused information rather than thirty pages padded out with irrelevance.

Create a positive image

Writing an effective CV involves a number of important aspects. One of those is the manner in which you present your CV. When developing your CV ask yourself the following questions:

- Are the spelling, grammar and punctuation correct?

- Is it legible and easy to read?

- Is the style in which you are writing your CV standardised?

- Is it neat?

- Is it constructed in a logical manner?

By following the above tips in respect of your CV image you will be on the right track, excuse the pun, to improving your chances of getting a job as a Railway Signaller. You should spend just as much time on the presentation of your CV as you do on the content.

Do you have the right qualities and attributes for the job you are applying for?

When you are developing your CV have a look at the required personal qualities that are listed within the job/person spec. Try to match these as closely as possible but again, ensure that you provide examples where appropriate.

Be honest when creating your CV

If you lie on your CV, especially when it comes to academic qualifications or experience, you will almost certainly get caught out at some point in the future. Maybe not straight away but even a few months or years down the line an employer can still dismiss you for incorrect information that you provide during the selection process. It simply isn't worth it. Be honest when creating your CV and if you don't have the right skills for the job you are applying for, then go out there and get them!

Now that I've shown you how to create an effective CV, schedule into your action plan a date and time when you intend to create your own. Now let's move on to how to complete the application form correctly.

CHAPTER FOUR

HOW TO COMPLETE
THE APPLICATION FORM

THE APPLICATION FORM

The types of questions that you will be asked to respond to on the application form can vary in nature. However, the questions and response I have provided within this section of your guide will be a fantastic starting point. Within this section of the guide I have also provided you with hints, tips and advice on how to increase your chances of progressing through this important stage. Follow the guidance that I have provided you within this section and your chances will greatly increase. Network Rail will normally require you to complete the application form online.

PREPARING TO COMPLETE THE APPLICATION FORM

Most of the sections on the application form are relatively straightforward to complete. However, there are a number of

very important sections that will need your utmost attention if you are to succeed. First of all, read the following tips and advice that relate to the completion of your application form:

Read everything first

This applies to both the application form, the accompanying literature (if any) and the Network Rail website. You will need to understand a little bit about the company first before you can successfully complete the application form. You should also study the job description, person specification and the accompanying recruitment guidance notes. Network Rail will also require you to read thoroughly the document entitled "A day in the life of a Railway Signaller". This document can be downloaded from the Network Rail website.

Correct ink colour

In the unlikely event that you are asked to complete a paper-based application form, make sure you read any requirements that relate to ink colour or capital letters etc. The recruitment office will receive many applications for every job advertised and the initial sift will look at minor errors such as these. If you cannot follow simple instructions, such as the correct ink colour, then there is not much chance you'll be able to concentrate properly as a Railway Signaller! Read everything carefully and follow ALL instructions.

Complete a rough draft first

The first time around you are more than likely to make mistakes. I advise that you photocopy the application form first (unless you are completing an on-line version) and complete a rough draft first. This will give you the opportunity to practice. Then, once you have finished your application, take a copy of it so that you can refer to it before you attend the interview. The interview panel will most certainly refer to your application form and your CV during the interview.

Before you complete the form you may get asked a number of questions to assess your eligibility for the role. Here are a few examples of the types of questions you might get asked:

EXAMPLES OF ELIGIBILITY QUESTIONS ('YES' ANSWERS REQUIRED)

1. I understand that I will be required to work all kinds of shifts

2. I understand that there is a stringent drugs and alcohol policy and I will take part in pre-employment and on the job drugs screening in addition to a medical assessment including a colour blindness test

3. I know that I could be working with computers

4. I understand that the training may be residential, lasts for several weeks and that I will need to learn a lot of rules and procedures

5. I accept that I will have responsibility for ensuring the safety of other rail industry employees and the general public

6. I am aware that I may be either working on my own for long periods of time or closely with others in a box

7. I understand that I will need to take a series of tests as part of the selection process

8. I am aware that incidents involving physical injuries or fatalities may occur on the railway, and if they do that I will be required to play a role

On the following pages I have provided you with a number of sample responses to some of the more common types

of application form question. The 'question and answer' sections on the application form are very important and represent an opportunity for you to show the recruitment staff how good you are. Before each question I have explained what the question means and how best to construct your response to it. Then, I have provided a sample response to each question. Please note that these are to be used as a guide only. I cannot guarantee that these questions will appear on your application; however, they are great practise for the real thing!

SAMPLE QUESTION NUMBER 1

Now that you've read more about the job, please tell us why you're applying for it and what knowledge, experience or skills you have that might be relevant.

The clue in this type of question is to READ about the job you are applying for. The question is asking you to match your knowledge, experience and skills with the job you have applied for. Therefore, you need to read the job description before responding. Job descriptions or person specifications usually have both 'essential' and 'desirable' criteria included. Basically you must provide evidence of where you can meet the 'essential' criteria on your application form. Desirable criteria will gain you extra marks but they are not essential.

If Network Rail have not sent you a copy of the job description then try to obtain a copy of it before completing the form. This will give you an insight into the role that you are applying for. Once you have read the information about the post you will then be able to construct your answer. Try to include any knowledge, skills or experience you may have that relates to the job description. If you have experience or knowledge in health and safety, working in pressurised situations or working in a customer-based environment then you may wish to include these also.

Now take a look at the following sample response before constructing your own, based on your own skills, knowledge and experience.

SAMPLE RESPONSE TO QUESTION NUMBER 1

I am applying for this post because I am looking for a new and challenging role. I enjoy working in a safety-critical environment and believe I would make an excellent Railway Signaller for your company. I am also prepared to relocate to live within the required distance of my place of work, if required. I understand that the company is changing and moving forward and I believe you would be an exciting company to work for. I also believe I can bring something to the team in terms of commitment, motivation, flexibility and enthusiasm.

I have worked in safety-critical roles for a number of years now and during this time I have developed skills that can be applied to the role of a Signaller. As well as being a good communicator and possessing excellent organisational skills, I am also highly safety-conscious and understand that this is a very important element of the role. In addition to my 12 years' experience in a civilian role, I also worked for the Royal Navy for 4 years. I am therefore a highly disciplined person and a very good team player. I have educational qualifications in English Language, English Literature and Art and I am also coming to the end of studying for a Diploma in Management Studies. I also hold a Health and Safety qualification through IODA in Nottingham. I am a fit and active person who visits the gym/swimming pool three times a week and I also play football for a local Sunday team. I am a very good communicator and learn new skills quickly. I am used to working long and varied hours and I understand that the role requires a high level of flexibility, which I am prepared for. I enjoy working with, and meeting people from all walks of life and I truly value the benefits of a diverse workforce. To summarise, I am a highly professional, caring, trustworthy, friendly and motivated person and I believe I would make an excellent member of the Network Rail Signalling team.

SAMPLE QUESTION NUMBER 2

Please tell us about anything you get up to outside work that gives us a better idea of what you're like as a person and why you might be right for our company. Please give the name of the activity and what it says about you.

This type of question is designed to assess the type of person you are outside of work. This will give the company an idea of how you are likely to perform at work and will tell them if you are fit, healthy and active. When responding to this type of question, make sure you make reference to the job description. What type of duties will you be required to perform and can you match your external activities to them? Being fit and active is always a positive aspect that the recruitment staff will be looking for. If you are active outside of work, then you are also likely to be active at work and achieve your tasks to the required standard. If you have recently achieved any educational or academic qualifications outside of work then it would be a good idea to make reference to these too. Now take a look at the sample response before creating your own based around your own skills, knowledge and experience.

SAMPLE RESPONSE TO QUESTION NUMBER 2

KEEPING FIT – I attend the gym at least 3 times per week and carry out some light weight work. Whilst at the gym, I usually perform 20 minutes of rowing each time and cover a distance of 5,000 metres. I particularly enjoy swimming and swim 50 lengths, 3 times per week. When I get the opportunity, I like to go walking, too, in order to keep healthy. Staying fit and healthy means that I am able to maintain a high level of concentration at work and it also helps to keep my enthusiasm and motivation levels high. This shows that I am a dedicated and determined person who is always looking to improve himself.

MUSICIAN – I currently play the drums and piano. I have always enjoyed being creative and I play the drums in a function band that plays at wedding events and parties on some weekends. This shows that I have the dedication to learn new skills and I have the ability to concentrate on the task in hand when required. Learning new skills is essential to the role of a Signaller and I believe that I have the ability to learn new skills quickly and adapt them to the work environment in a safe and effective manner.

SAMPLE QUESTION NUMBER 3

As the role you've applied for means that you'll be dealing with the safety of our customers and the delivery of our operation, we would like to hear examples of how you have used your initiative to solve a difficult problem.

Having the initiative to react quickly and solve difficult problems is integral to the Signallers role. On many occasions you will be on your own in the signal box and you will have to deal with sometimes difficult and challenging situations. Whilst you will have set procedures and guidelines to adhere to, you must still have the required initiative to solve difficult problems. Before responding to questions of this nature, make sure you READ the question first and try to understand what is required. Remember to write a response that identifies the use of your initiative to solve a difficult problem.

SAMPLE RESPONSE TO QUESTION NUMBER 3

During a recent staff meeting I was aware that there were a number of problems between some members of the team. The team wasn't working effectively so we all discussed ways in which we could improve. The actions of the team were starting to have an effect on the team's performance, so I decided to take the initiative to resolve the issue. I facilitated the meeting and asked everybody to share their views and opinions. I listened to each person individually and tried to encourage people to come up with solutions in order to improve the team's effectiveness. A positive point that came from our discussions was that people felt that we didn't hold enough meetings to talk about the problems we all face. It was agreed that with immediate effect we would hold weekly meetings to discuss issues, gather and share information, and look for ways that we could all support each other in our work. Since the meeting the team has moved forward and is now working far more effectively.

SAMPLE QUESTION NUMBER 4

As the role you've applied for means that you'll be dealing with the safety of our customers and the delivery of our operation, we would like to hear examples of how you have played a positive role as team member or leader.

Having the ability to work as an effective team member is important in any organisation and Network Rail are no exception. The organisation will be made up of many different people, all of whom have an important role to perform. Therefore, it is essential that you have had some experience of working in a team environment, either as a team member or team leader. Try to think of an occasion when you have been part of a team or have even been the leader of a team. When responding to questions of this nature, think of a scenario where you worked as part of the team to achieve a task or solve a problem. Now take a look at the following sample response before using blank sheet of paper to construct your own.

SAMPLE RESPONSE TO QUESTION NUMBER 4

In my current role, I am responsible for the safety of my team and for ensuring that any health and safety incidents are reported in line with company regulations. I am also involved in coaching and mentoring my team and providing them with feedback, often helping them to improve. I currently lead a team of 18 staff and I am required to ensure the team operates effectively in terms of management, health and safety, and training. Following any incident that relates to health and safety I always fully brief each member of the team to ensure that I have done everything in my power to prevent an incident occurring again.

SAMPLE QUESTION NUMBER 5

As the role you've applied for means that you'll be dealing with the safety of our customers and the delivery of our operation, we would like to hear examples of how you have had to work under pressure.

If you are successful in your pursuit of becoming a Railway Signaller, you will undoubtedly be presented with scenarios and situations where you have to remain calm and focused and this question is designed to assess your ability to do just that. Try to think of a scenario where you have worked under pressure but still achieved the task or goal.

Take a look at the following sample response before using a blank sheet of paper to construct your own response based on your own experiences.

SAMPLE RESPONSE TO QUESTION NUMBER 5

In my current role as customer service manager I am required to work under pressure on a daily basis. Recently, I was presented with a situation where two members of staff had gone sick leaving me with only three other staff members to manage the shop during a busy Saturday.

During the morning we were due to take a stock delivery which meant that I had to perform many tasks without taking a break. During the day I dealt with two customer complaints, took delivery of the stock, served customers whilst others took their break and also dealt with a fire alarm actuation. I am often required to perform under pressure and thrive in such conditions. I always adapt well to situations like these and ensure that I still maintain a high level of professionalism at all times.

SAMPLE QUESTION NUMBER 6

As the role you've applied for means that you'll be dealing with the safety of our customers and the delivery of our operation, we would like to hear examples of how you have taken responsibility to communicate an important message.

As a Railway Signaller you will have to communicate important messages to other members of the rail team, such as train drivers. The messages may relate to delays along the track or incidents that are occurring up ahead. Try to think of an occasion where you have had to communicate an important message where you were under pressure. Take a look at the following sample response which will help you to create your own. Once you have read the provided example, use a blank sheet of paper to construct your own response based on your own experiences.

SAMPLE RESPONSE TO QUESTION NUMBER 6

Whilst working in my current position as a sales person I was the duty manager for the day as my manager had gone sick. It was the week before Christmas and the shop was very busy. During the day the fire alarm went off and I started to ask everybody to evacuate the shop, which is our company policy. The alarm has gone off in the past but the normal manager usually lets people stay in the shop whilst he finds out if it's a false alarm. This was a difficult situation because the shop was very busy, nobody wanted to leave, and my shop assistants were disagreeing with me in my decision to evacuate the shop. Some of the customers were becoming irate as they were in the changing rooms at the time. Both the customers and my shop assistants were disagreeing with me. The customers were saying that it was appalling that they had to evacuate the shop and that they would complain to the head office about it. My sales staff were trying to persuade me to keep everybody inside the shop and that it was most probably a false alarm, like it usually is. I was determined to evacuate everybody from the shop for safety reasons and would not allow anybody to deter me from my aim. The safety of my staff and customers was at the forefront of my mind, even though it wasn't at theirs. I persisted with my actions and eventually got everybody to leave the shop. When the Fire Service arrived they informed me that there had been a small fire at the rear of the shop and that the actions I had taken were the right ones. Everybody was safe and nobody was hurt as a result of the incident.

SAMPLE QUESTION NUMBER 7

Please give details of any personal development you have undertaken.

You may get asked this question on the application form as the role of a Railway Signaller requires an ability to continually develop and learn new skills. Take a look at the following sample response which will help you to gain an understanding of what is required.

SAMPLE RESPONSE TO QUESTION NUMBER 7

Although I am in my late thirties I had always wanted to learn to play the guitar. It is something that I have wanted to do for many years, but have never had the time to learn until recently. One day I was watching a band play with my wife at my local pub and decided there and then that I would make it my mission to learn to play competently. The following day I went onto the internet and searched for a good guitar tutor in my local area. Luckily, I managed to find one within my town who had a very good reputation for teaching. I immediately booked a block of lessons and started my first one within a week. My development in the use of playing the guitar progressed rapidly and I soon achieved grade 1 standard. Every night of the week I would dedicate at least 30 minutes of time to my learning, in addition to my one hour weekly lesson. I soon found that I was progressing through the grades quickly, which was due to my level of learning commitment and a desire to become competent in playing the instrument. I recently achieved level 4 and I am now working to level 5 standard. I am also now playing in a local band and the opportunities for me, both musically and socially, have increased tenfold since learning to play. In addition to this, learning to play the guitar has improved my concentration levels and my patience. I am always looking to improve myself and I am very keen on continuous personal development.

SAMPLE QUESTION NUMBER 8

Please give an example of when you have provided excellent customer service.

It goes without saying that, in order to become a great Railway Signaller you will need to provide excellent service. Take a look at the following sample response to this question.

SAMPLE RESPONSE TO QUESTION NUMBER 8

Whilst working as a shop assistant in my current role, a member of the public came in to complain about a pair of football shoes that he had bought for his son's birthday. When his son came to open the present on the morning of his birthday, he noticed that one of the football boots was a larger size than the other. He was supposed to be playing football with his friends that morning and wanted to wear his new boots. However, due to the shop's mistake, this was not possible. Naturally, the boy was very upset.

I remained calm throughout and listened to the gentleman very carefully, showing complete empathy for his son's situation. This immediately defused any potential confrontation. Once I had listened to his complaint I then told him how sorry I was for the mistake that had happened, and that I would feel exactly the same if it was my own son who it had happened to. I then told the gentleman that I would refund the money in full and give his son a new pair of football boots to the same value as the previous pair.

The man was delighted with my offer and resolution to the complaint. Not only that, I then offered to give the man a further discount of 10% on any future purchase, due to the added inconvenience that was caused by him having to return to the shop to sort out the problem. I believe customer service is very important in any work-related role, as it is the customer that keeps the business profitable. The potential for losing a customer was averted by my actions and I felt sure the man would return to our shop again.

SAMPLE QUESTION NUMBER 9

Please give details of when you have dealt with a difficult situation.

As a Railway Signaller you will be required to take responsibility for dealing with difficult situations. It might be trespassers on the track or perhaps even a fatality that you have to deal with. This question is designed to see whether or not you have any experience of taking responsibility for difficult situations and, more importantly, resolving them.

SAMPLE RESPONSE TO QUESTION NUMBER 9

One evening I was sat at home watching television when I heard my next door neighbours smoke alarm sounding. This is not an unusual occurrence as she is always setting off the alarm whilst cooking. However, on this occasion, something was different as the alarm did not normally sound so late at night. I got up out of my chair and went to see if she was OK. She is a vulnerable, elderly lady and I always look out for her whenever possible. When I arrived next door I peered through the window and noticed my neighbour sat asleep on the chair in the front room. Wisps of smoke were coming from kitchen so I knew that she was in trouble. I immediately ran back into my house and dialled 999 calmly. I asked for the Fire Service and the Ambulance Service and explained that a person was stuck inside the house with a fire burning in the kitchen. I provided the call operator as much information as possible including landmarks close to our road to make it easier for the Fire Service to find. As soon as I got off the phone I immediately went round the back of my house to climb over the fence. Mrs Watson, my neighbour, usually leaves her back door unlocked until she goes to bed. I climbed over the fence and tried the door handle. Thankfully the door opened. I entered into the kitchen and turned off the gas heat which was burning dried up soup. I then ran to the front room, woke up Mrs Watson and carried her carefully through the front door, as this was the nearest exit. I then sat Mrs Watson down on the pavement outside and placed my coat around her. It wasn't long before the Fire Service arrived and they took over from them on in. I gave them all of the details relating to the incident and informed them of my actions when in the kitchen.

SAMPLE QUESTION NUMBER 10

Please give details of when your communications skills made a difference to a situation.

Being able to communicate effectively is crucial to the role of a Railway Signaller. Not only will you have to communicate with your colleagues and supervisors, but you will also have to give important messages to the train drivers. Take a look at the following sample response to this question.

SAMPLE RESPONSE TO QUESTION NUMBER 10

My next door neighbour had a cat they had looked after for years and they were very fond of it. I had to inform them that their cat had just been run over by a car in the road. I was fully aware of how much they loved their cat and I could understand that the message I was about to tell them would have been deeply distressing. They had cherished the cat for years and to suddenly lose it would have been a great shock to them. To begin with I knocked at their door and ask calmly if I could come in to speak to them. Before I broke the news to them I made them a cup of tea and sat them down in a quiet room away from any distractions. I then carefully and sensitively told them that their cat had passed away following an accident in the road. At all times I took into account their feelings and I made sure I delivered the message sensitively and in a caring manner. I took into account where and when I was going to deliver the message. It was important to tell them in a quiet room away from any distractions so that they could grieve in peace. I also took into account the tone in which I delivered the message and I also made sure that I was sensitive to their feelings. I also made sure that I would be available to support them after I had broken the news. I strongly believe that the manner in which I communicated and delivered the message was helpful to the already difficult situation.

FINAL TIPS FOR CREATING A SUCCESSFUL APPLICATION FORM

- Read the form carefully before starting to complete it. Also be sure to read all of the accompanying guidance notes, person specification and job description.

- Follow all instructions carefully. Your form can be rejected for failing to follow simple instructions.

- If you are completing a handwritten version of the form make sure your handwriting is neat, legible, concise and grammatically correct. You will lose marks for incorrect spelling!

- Before you submit the form get somebody to check over it for you.

- Once you have completed the form make sure you make a photocopy of it. You may be asked questions that relate to your responses during the interview.

- Send the form recorded delivery if completing a paper-based version. I have known of many application forms to go missing in the post.

CHAPTER FIVE

THE ASSESSMENT CENTRE AND SAMPLE TESTS

The assessment centre is designed specifically to help Network Rail select the best people for the job. You will be asked to sit a number of tests and exercises in order to prove your competence in the different assessment areas. People who do well at the assessment centre tend to do well in the Railway Signaller role itself. Within this section, I have provided you with practice tests that will improve the skills and qualities needed to become a Railway Signaller. *Please note that these tests are not the actual assessments, they are merely designed by How2become to ensure you with the best practice*. Where necessary, I have also indicated where you can find alternative or additional testing resources to help improve your performance.

ON ARRIVAL AT THE ASSESSMENT CENTRE

When you arrive at the centre, the centre manager or assessment centre administrator will check your forms of identification and also take any pictures they requested off you before confirming your name and address etc. They will then usually split you up into groups, if there are a large number of applicants. The room where you will be taking the assessments will be set up like a classroom with tables and chairs. This is the room where you will sit the paper-based exams/tests. They will ask everyone to switch off all mobile phones and pagers and to also remove your jackets and coats. You will also be asked if you are fit and able to undertake the tests.

You will then normally be supplied with spare paper to do any working outs on and also a rubber, pen or pencil in order to complete the assessments with. For your comfort you will also be supplied with a glass or bottle of water for you to drink if you wish. The administrator will then go into detail and explain what will be happening during the assessment centre and also the usual health and safety requirements. Let's now take a look at each of the different testing areas.

THE SITUATIONAL JUDGEMENT TEST (SJT)

The SJT consists of 16 scenarios. They each present a situation with 3 possible responses. You are asked to indicate whether you believe the response to be the most effective; the next most effective; or the least effective response. There is no time limit to this test. However, try not to spend too long thinking about each one. The test should take you about 20 minutes.

The following scenario shows an example of the sorts of statements you will see. Have a go at doing the example.

SAMPLE SITUATIONAL JUDGEMENT TEST QUESTION

You are in a situation where first aid is required. Everyone at the company has had basic first aid training, and a colleague of yours has had a seizure. Nobody wants to help because they are unsure of how to proceed.

Do you:

A. Ask one of your colleagues to help whilst you phone for an ambulance.

B. Put your colleague in the recovery position and wait for help.

C. Remain calm, get someone to call for an ambulance, and reassure your colleague whilst holding their head so they don't cause more injury.

ANSWERS:

MOST EFFECTIVE =

NEXT MOST EFFECTIVE =

LEAST EFFECTIVE =

Within this particular question, the **MOST EFFECTIVE** answer would be C. The reason for this is because the situation requires a strong awareness of health and safety. Remaining calm and ensuring help is on its way is the best way to deal with this situation.

The **NEXT MOST EFFECTIVE** answer is A. Ensuring that someone remains with the colleague has had a seizure is practical. Whereas the **LEAST EFFECTIVE** answer is answer B. You should be aware not to move a person after a seizure to ensure further damage is not caused.

Now try the following 6 sample Situational Judgement Test questions to see how you get on.

6 SAMPLE SITUATIONAL JUDGEMENT TEST QUESTIONS

Q1. A work colleague at the train station has been absent due to sickness and she has missed an important operational incident debrief that has highlighted a number of important changes to rail signalling procedures. What would you do?

Please pick the MOST EFFECTIVE answer, the NEXT MOST EFFECTIVE answer and the LEAST EFFECTIVE answer in terms of what you should do.

A. Immediately explain to her what the changes are and clarify that she fully understands them.

B. Inform your line manager of her absence so that he can tell her there and then what they are.

C. Do nothing. She will probably find out about the changes through other work colleagues or whilst she is on the job.

D. Wait until the following day before you inform her. There'll be more time then to explain what the changes are.

YOUR ANSWERS:

MOST EFFECTIVE =

NEXT MOST EFFECTIVE =

LEAST EFFECTIVE =

Q2. During an incident the Signal Box manager gives you instructions to immediately stop what you are doing and communicate an important message to the Rail Control Centre (RCC). Once you have received the instructions, what would you do?

Please pick the MOST EFFECTIVE answer, the NEXT MOST EFFECTIVE answer and the LEAST EFFECTIVE answer in terms of what you should do.

A. Finish off the entire shift before contacting the RCC to pass on the message.

B. Immediately stop what I am doing if safe to do so before contacting the RCC to communicate the message. Once I have communicated the message, and confirmed that the RCC fully understands it, I will then inform the Signal Box manager that the message has been sent. I would then return to my previous task.

C. Because I am already involved in another task, I will pass the message onto another Railway Signaller so that he/she can communicate the message to the RCC.

D. Immediately stop what I am doing if safe to do so before contacting the RCC to communicate the message. Once I have communicated the message, I will then inform the Signal Box manager that the message has been sent. I would then return to my previous task.

YOUR ANSWERS:

MOST EFFECTIVE =

NEXT MOST EFFECTIVE =

LEAST EFFECTIVE =

Q3. A team meeting has been held at the train station but you were unable to attend due to sickness. The next day you are back at work and you ask a colleague what happened at the meeting. She informs you that you missed nothing and that the meeting was very boring. What would you do?

Please pick the MOST EFFECTIVE answer, the NEXT MOST EFFECTIVE answer and the LEAST EFFECTIVE answer in terms of what you should do.

A. I would take her word for it. Most meetings are quite boring.

B. I would ask my manager what happened at the meeting the next time I see him.

C. I would persist and ask her to tell me what went on at the meeting.

D. Wait to be told by someone else what happened at the meeting.

YOUR ANSWERS:

MOST EFFECTIVE =

NEXT MOST EFFECTIVE =

LEAST EFFECTIVE =

Q4. You are at work in the Signal Box when your manager asks you to order some operational incident reporting sheets as she is busy. You go online to order the sheets and one of the more experienced Railway Signallers tells you not to bother as there are plenty in the storeroom. What do you do?

Please pick the MOST EFFECTIVE answer, the NEXT MOST EFFECTIVE answer and the LEAST EFFECTIVE answer in terms of what you should do.

A. Order the leaflets as I have been told to do so.

B. Politely tell the experienced Signaller to leave me alone, I have a job to do!

C. Take his advice. After all he's been in the job for years, so he must be right.

D. Check in the storeroom first to see if there are sufficient leaflets. If there were not, then I'd order them. If there were sufficient leaflets, then I would inform my manager.

YOUR ANSWERS:

MOST EFFECTIVE =

NEXT MOST EFFECTIVE =

LEAST EFFECTIVE =

Q5. Whilst carrying out a morning training session at work you notice that you are not familiar with a new operational rail procedure that has been issued. What would you do?

Please pick the MOST EFFECTIVE answer, the NEXT MOST EFFECTIVE answer and the LEAST EFFECTIVE answer in terms of what you should do.

A. Not worry about it as there will be another signaller who knows more about it than me.

B. Read the instruction manual on the new operational rail procedure over a cup of tea at lunchtime.

C. Schedule in some time over the next few days to read it when I have the time.

D. Take immediate steps to make sure that I become familiar with the new operational rail procedure and that I fully understand it.

YOUR ANSWERS:

MOST EFFECTIVE =

NEXT MOST EFFECTIVE =

LEAST EFFECTIVE =

Q6. You are sat around the lunch table having a cup of tea with the rest of the Railway Signallers at the end of your shift. There's a bit of banter going on and one of the more senior Railway Signallers is making fun out of a new member of your team and is starting to make discriminatory comments. The new member of the team appears to be slightly upset by the comments but doesn't say anything. What would you do?

Please pick the MOST EFFECTIVE answer, the NEXT MOST EFFECTIVE answer and the LEAST EFFECTIVE answer in terms of what you should do.

A. I would intervene to put a stop to the comments, explaining that I didn't think the comments were appropriate. Even though the member of the team is new, that doesn't mean he or she should be the centre of any harmful jokes or comments.

B. Banter is all part and parcel of life within the Rail Industry. Railway Signallers work together in sometimes stressful situations and a bit of banter is good for morale. If the new member of the team is going to fit in, then he/she will need to get used to it.

C. I would leave the room and go and inform my line manager of the comments.

D. I would probably join in with the banter.

YOUR ANSWERS:

MOST EFFECTIVE =

NEXT MOST EFFECTIVE =

LEAST EFFECTIVE =

ANSWERS TO 6 SAMPLE SITUATIONAL JUDGEMENT TEST QUESTIONS

Q1.   MOST EFFECTIVE = A
NEXT MOST EFFECTIVE = B
LEAST EFFECTIVE = C

Q2.   MOST EFFECTIVE = B
NEXT MOST EFFECTIVE = D
LEAST EFFECTIVE = A

Q3.   MOST EFFECTIVE = C
NEXT MOST EFFECTIVE = B
LEAST EFFECTIVE = A

Q4.   MOST EFFECTIVE = A
NEXT MOST EFFECTIVE = B
LEAST EFFECTIVE = C

Q5.   MOST EFFECTIVE = D
NEXT MOST EFFECTIVE = B
LEAST EFFECTIVE = A

Q6.   MOST EFFECTIVE = A
NEXT MOST EFFECTIVE = C
LEAST EFFECTIVE = D

If you would like to try more Situational Judgment Test questions please go to:

www.SituationalJudgmentTest.co.uk

OBSERVATIONAL ABILITY TEST (OAT)

During this particular stage of the assessment they are interested in your concentration and attention on a range of everyday tasks. The test will be administered in a group setting and will take approximately 50 minutes.

Below are the types of tests you may be asked to take:

1. The Map Search

2. Lift Counting

3. Lift Counting with Reversal

4. Telephone Directory Search

5. Telephone Search with Dual Task

6. Lottery Ticket Task

This particular test is an excellent predictor of effective signaller performance as candidates undertaking the assessment need to focus, do more than one thing at a time, sustain attention on a relatively repetitive task and respond to auditory and visual information.

Some of the tests are designed to be particularly challenging, particularly when it is assessing your multi-task capacity, and so even as an experienced signaller you are not expected to get everything correct. The cut offs for this test are set specifically to identify whether people may have attentional deficits.

The Map Search

The first task involves searching a map and crossing off a particular symbol on the map when located. There is a 2-minute time limit, so you will have to work quickly but accurately.

To help you prepare for the Map Search test please try to locate the following London underground Tube Stations on the following 5 maps. Answers are supplied at the end of the exercise. You have just 2 minutes to complete all 5 questions.

MAP SEARCH QUESTION 1

Locate and draw a circle around the following stations:
Wembley Park and Golders Green

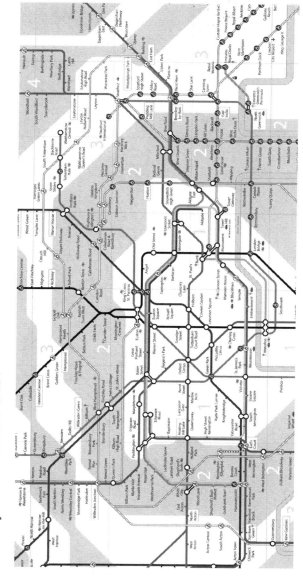

MAP SEARCH QUESTION 2

Locate and draw a circle around the following stations:

Regent's Park and Euston

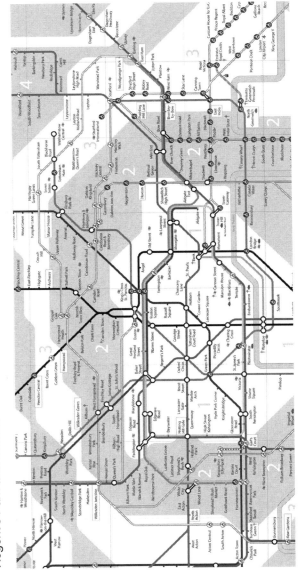

MAP SEARCH QUESTION 3

Locate and draw a circle around the following stations:

Gloucester Road and Highgate

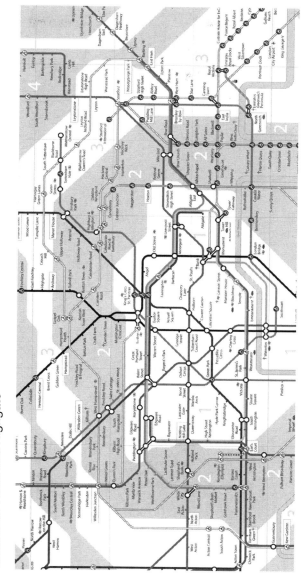

MAP SEARCH QUESTION 4

Locate and draw a circle around the following stations:

Swiss Cottage and Kilburn

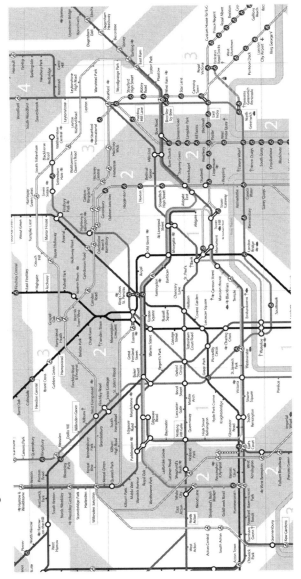

MAP SEARCH QUESTION 5

Locate and draw a circle around the following stations:

Great Portland Street and Angel

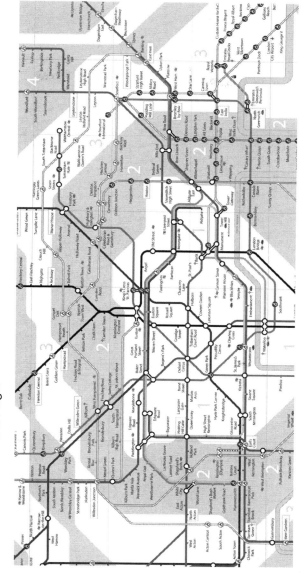

ANSWER TO MAP SEARCH QUESTION 1

Locate and draw a circle around the following stations:
Wembley Park and Golders Green

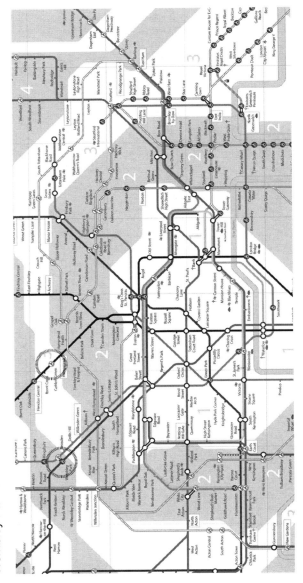

ANSWER TO MAP SEARCH QUESTION 2

Locate and draw a circle around the following stations:
Regent's Park and Euston

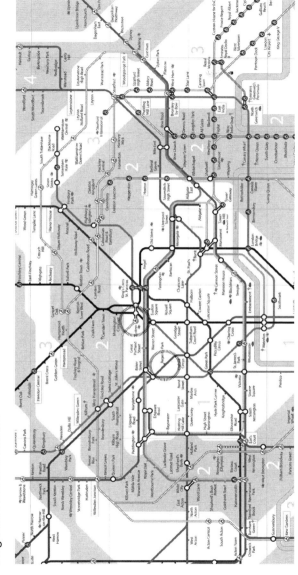

ANSWER TO MAP SEARCH QUESTION 3

Locate and draw a circle around the following stations:
Gloucester Road and Highgate

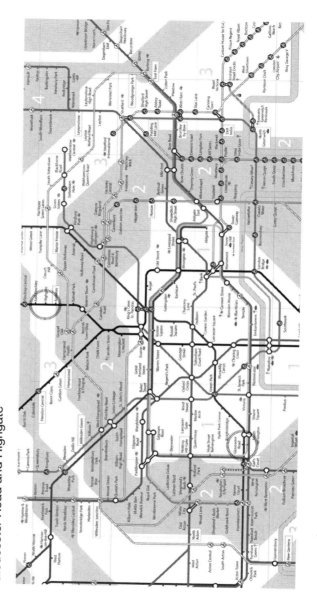

ANSWER TO MAP SEARCH QUESTION 4

Locate and draw a circle around the following stations:
Swiss Cottage and Kilburn

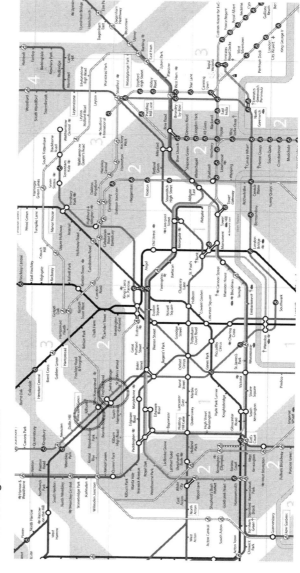

ANSWER TO MAP SEARCH QUESTION 5

Locate and draw a circle around the following stations:

Great Portland Street and Angel

Lift Counting

The second task involves listening to an audio CD, representing the tones of a lift in your hotel as it passes different floors. You must count a tone of a particular frequency, while ignoring the distracting tone of a different pitch. You will be asked to write down how many tones you have heard representing how many floors you have travelled in the lift.

Lift Counting with Reversal

The third task is similar to the second task, but this time, there will be three (3) differing tones and you are asked to imagine that you are still in your hotel lift and it is travelling both upwards and downwards. You know whether the lift is going up or down by the sounds played on the CD. There are three types of sounds:

1. The middle-pitched tone which corresponds to a "floor". This tone needs to be counted.

2. The high-pitched tone which corresponds to "up" and means that the lift has stopped and is now going to go up.

3. The low-pitched tone which corresponds to "down" and means that the lift has stopped and is now going to go down.

You must count the floor tones but at the same time listen carefully so you know which direction the lift is travelling in. You will be asked to write down what floor the lift stops at.

Telephone Directory Search

The fourth task involves reading through a telephone directory and pinpointing all the information that contains the same area code and symbol. This tests specifically assesses your attention to detail, as well as test your concentration levels and time skills.

 how2become

Telephone Directory Search with Dual Task

The fifth task is another search of the telephone directory but this time is performed in combination with a second task – counting strings of tones presented on an audio CD. You must put equal effort into each of the two simultaneous tasks.

Lottery Ticket Task

The final task sets the scene that you have bought lottery tickets and you are listening to an announcement of winning tickets. You need to listen to a series of letters and numbers that always begin with two letters and end with three numbers. For example, a voice will say: 'E-F-1-8-4'. You must to listen for tickets ending in 5-5. When you hear a number ending in 5-5, you must write down the first two letters of that ticket on the sheet provided. For example, GH-3-5-5, you would write GH.

TRAIN DRIVER ERROR CHECKING TEST (TD-ECT)

During your Train Driver assessment, you will be expected to take a test that is designed to assess the key skills and qualities required by anyone who wishes to become a Railway Signaller or Train Driver. As an aspiring Train Driver, you will need to demonstrate high levels of skills in the following areas:

- Concentration
- Attention to detail
- Awareness
- Perseverance

The Train Driver Error Checking Test (TD-ECT) is a test primarily designed to assess these particular areas in order to improve your overall performance. Created by How2become, this Train Driver practice test allows you to practice and prepare for your assessment. *Please note, that whilst we have provided practice questions, the Train Driver Error Checking Test (TD-ECT) is not an official Train Driving test.* It is a test created by our team for you to gain a clearer understanding of the nature of the test, and the typical skills that are often evaluated.

ABOUT THE TRAIN DRIVER ERROR CHECKING TEST (TD-ECT)

The Train Driver Error Checking Test is an assessment that allows aspiring Railway Signallers and Train Drivers to practice their skills in order to prepare them for their assessment. The test measures particular skills, particularly focussing on concentration ability and attention to detail. These skills will be put to the test by measuring a person's ability to recognise errors in diagram formations.

Becoming a Railway Signaller requires a great deal of perseverance, and much of that perseverance comes from practicing.

The more a person practices prior to their assessment, the more comfortable and confident they will feel in regards to their test. Thus, it is imperative that, whilst we cannot provide an exact account of what to expect in your actual test, we can provide questions that will focus on the necessary skills and qualities Train Drivers and Railway Signallers must possess in order to be successful during the selection process.

The Error Code Chart will remain the same throughout the test, and is shown below:

You will then be given 6 questions based on an Error Reference Chart. This will need to be used and remembered to determine which errors the bicycles have. The bicycles may have one or more errors. You will be able to work out the errors based on the reference codes and whether they are the same. If the bicycle does not have the same reference code, then there is an error.

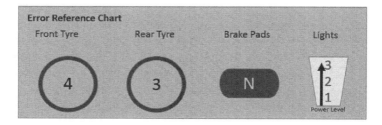

The Error Reference Chart is formulated above.

Using the Error Reference Chart, you must place the correct error code for each question. For Each Reference Chart, it will contain 5 questions. You will need to work out where the errors lie in the diagram.

Using the above Error Reference Chart, and using the Error Codes, find the error in the following diagram.

This is the order that you need to use to check each part of the bicycle. *The **Order for Checking** changes, so be sure to pay attention to this!*

Using the Error Codes (FT, RT, BP, L), you will need to put your answers in the report, in order of Checking, filling in the box where an error has occurred.

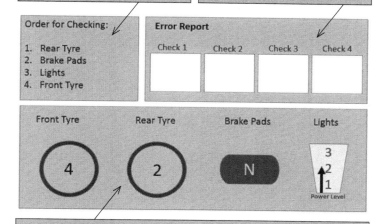

Order for Checking:

1. Rear Tyre
2. Brake Pads
3. Lights
4. Front Tyre

Error Report

Check 1	Check 2	Check 3	Check 4

Front Tyre: 4

Rear Tyre: 2

Brake Pads: N

Lights: Power Level 3 2 1

This set of diagrams need to be analysed carefully. You will have been given a Reference Chart to study before the question. Your task is to use that Reference Chart and cross-reference any errors in this set of diagrams. If a reference is different in the question, compared to that found on the Reference Chart, that means there is an error, and you would need to write it in the correct box in your report.

ANSWER FOR SAMPLE QUESTION

Error Report			
Check 1	Check 2	Check 3	Check 4
RT	–	**L**	–

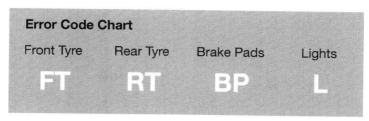

The above Chart is a reminder of the Error Codes that you will need to insert into the Error Report for each error you find.

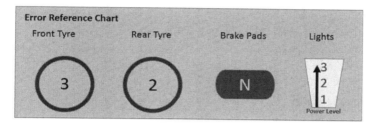

Using the Error Reference Chart above, *answer questions 1 to 6,* based on the information found in this chart.

For the **next 6 questions**, use the above Error Reference Chart to determine which errors the bicycle have. If the bicycle does not have the same reference, then there is an error.

Only enter a code if there is an error present! If an error is not present, draw a line through the box.

Question 1.

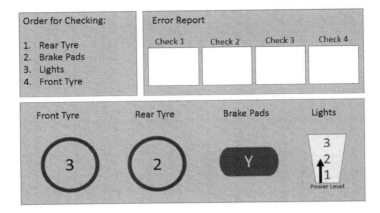

Question 2.

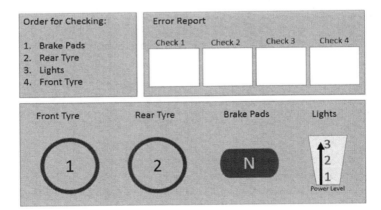

Question 3.

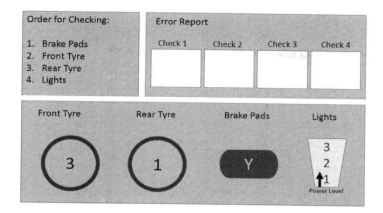

Question 4.

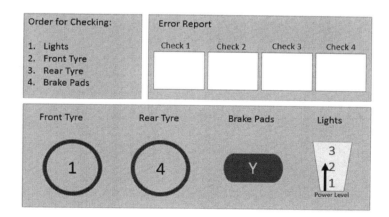

Question 5.

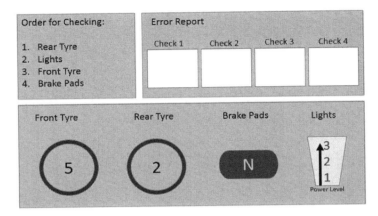

Question 6.

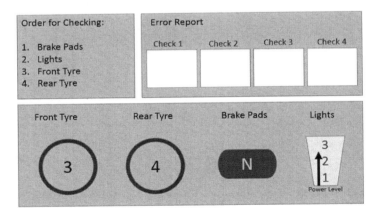

Error Code Chart

Front Tyre	Rear Tyre	Brake Pads	Lights
FT	RT	BP	L

The above Chart is a reminder of the Error Codes that you will need to insert into the Error Report for each error you find.

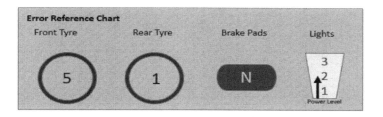

Error Reference Chart

Front Tyre	Rear Tyre	Brake Pads	Lights
5	1	N	3 / 2 / 1 Power Level

Using the Error Reference Chart above, *answer questions 7 to 12*, based on the information found in this chart.

For the **next 6 questions**, use the above Error Reference Chart to determine which errors the bicycle have. If the bicycle does not have the same reference, then there is an error.

Only enter a code if there is an error present! If an error is not present, draw a line through the box.

Question 7.

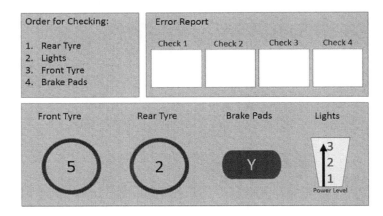

Question 8.

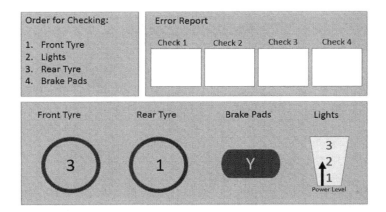

Question 9.

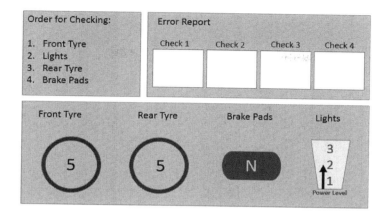

Question 10.

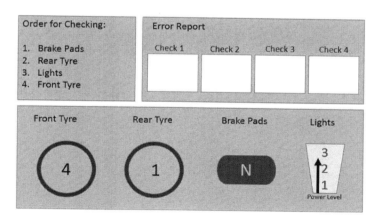

Question 11.

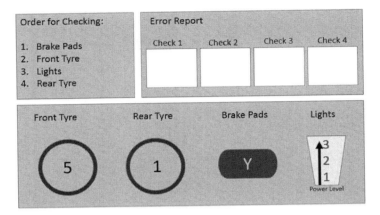

Question 12.

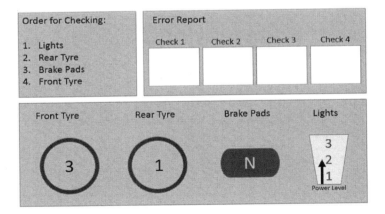

ANSWERS TO TRAIN DRIVER ERROR CHECKING TEST

Question 1.

Error Report			
Check 1	Check 2	Check 3	Check 4
—	**BP**	**L**	—

Question 2.

Error Report			
Check 1	Check 2	Check 3	Check 4
—	—	—	**FT**

Question 3.

Error Report			
Check 1	Check 2	Check 3	Check 4
BP	—	**RT**	**L**

Question 4.

Error Report			
Check 1	Check 2	Check 3	Check 4
L	FT	RT	BP

Question 5.

Error Report			
Check 1	Check 2	Check 3	Check 4
–	–	FT	–

Question 6.

Error Report			
Check 1	Check 2	Check 3	Check 4
–	L	–	RT

Question 7.

Error Report			
Check 1	Check 2	Check 3	Check 4
RT	**L**	**—**	**BP**

Question 8.

Error Report			
Check 1	Check 2	Check 3	Check 4
FT	**—**	**—**	**BP**

Question 9.

Error Report			
Check 1	Check 2	Check 3	Check 4
—	**—**	**RT**	**—**

Question 10.

Error Report			
Check 1	Check 2	Check 3	Check 4
—	—	L	FT

Question 11.

Error Report			
Check 1	Check 2	Check 3	Check 4
BP	—	L	—

Question 12.

Error Report			
Check 1	Check 2	Check 3	Check 4
—	—	—	FT

FURTHER CHECKING TESTS

In order to assist you in your preparation for the Checking Tests I have created further Checking Tests. Although the test is different to the test that you will encounter during the actual Railway Signaller tests, it will allow you to improve your skills in preparation for finding faults and errors which you will need to identify in your assessment.

In the following question you have to identify which of the three switches (W, Z or X) is not working. The box on the left hand side contains four circles, each labelled A, B, C and D. A key to the switches and the function they each perform is detailed below.

Q. Which switch in the sequence is not working?

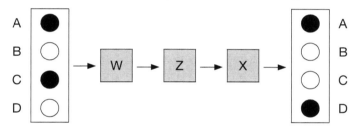

Switch	Function of the switch
W	Turns A and C on/off i.e. Black to white and vice versa
X	Turns B and D on/off i.e. Black to white and vice versa
Y	Turns C and D on/off i.e. Black to white and vice versa
Z	Turns A and D on/off i.e. Black to white and vice versa

You will notice that the box on the left contains black circles A and C, and white circles B and D at the start of the sequence.

The first switch to operate is 'W', which has the effect of turning circles A and C from black to white, and vice versa. Once switch 'W' operates, the lights on the left will all be white in colour.

The next switch to operate is switch Z, which has the effect of turning circles A and D from black to white and vice versa. Because the circles contained within the box on the left hand side are all white after the operation of switch W, this now means that circles A and D are black, and circles B and C are white. You will notice that the box with the four circles located on the right hand side is now identical to this, which means that switch X must be inoperative. If it was working correctly, then the box of circles on the right hand side would look different. Therefore the correct answer to the question is switch X.

Now that you understand what is required during this test, take the time to work through the following sample Checking Tests. You have 5 minutes to complete the 10 questions.

CHECKING TESTS

Q1. Which switch in the sequence is not working?

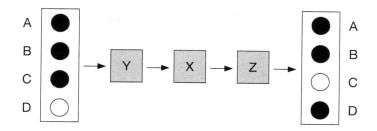

Switch	Function of the switch
W	Turns A and C on/off i.e. Black to white and vice versa
X	Turns B and D on/off i.e. Black to white and vice versa
Y	Turns C and D on/off i.e. Black to white and vice versa
Z	Turns A and D on/off i.e. Black to white and vice versa

Answer

Q2. Which switch in the sequence is not working?

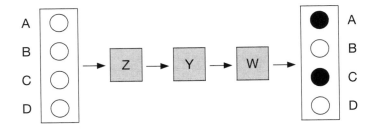

Switch	Function of the switch
W	Turns A and C on/off i.e. Black to white and vice versa
X	Turns B and D on/off i.e. Black to white and vice versa
Y	Turns C and D on/off i.e. Black to white and vice versa
Z	Turns A and D on/off i.e. Black to white and vice versa

Answer

Q3. Which switch in the sequence is not working?

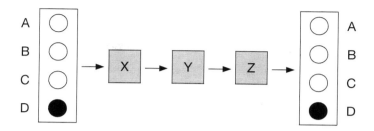

Switch	Function of the switch
W	Turns A and C on/off i.e. Black to white and vice versa
X	Turns B and D on/off i.e. Black to white and vice versa
Y	Turns C and D on/off i.e. Black to white and vice versa
Z	Turns A and D on/off i.e. Black to white and vice versa

Answer

Q4. Which switch in the sequence is not working?

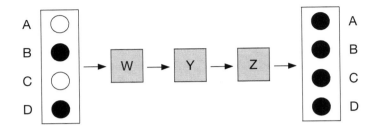

Switch	Function of the switch
W	Turns A and C on/off i.e. Black to white and vice versa
X	Turns B and D on/off i.e. Black to white and vice versa
Y	Turns C and D on/off i.e. Black to white and vice versa
Z	Turns A and D on/off i.e. Black to white and vice versa

Answer [   ]

how2become

Q5. Which switch in the sequence is not working?

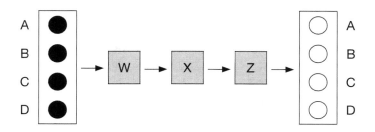

Switch	Function of the switch
W	Turns A and C on/off i.e. Black to white and vice versa
X	Turns B and D on/off i.e. Black to white and vice versa
Y	Turns C and D on/off i.e. Black to white and vice versa
Z	Turns A and D on/off i.e. Black to white and vice versa

Answer [   ]

Q6. Which switch in the sequence is not working?

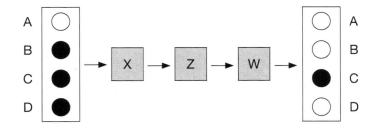

Switch	Function of the switch
W	Turns A and C on/off i.e. Black to white and vice versa
X	Turns B and D on/off i.e. Black to white and vice versa
Y	Turns C and D on/off i.e. Black to white and vice versa
Z	Turns A and D on/off i.e. Black to white and vice versa

Answer [   ]

Chapter Five The Assessment Centre and Sample Tests 105

Q7. Which switch in the sequence is not working?

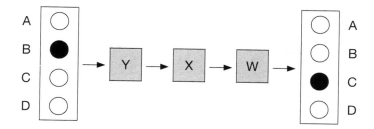

Switch	Function of the switch
W	Turns A and C on/off i.e. Black to white and vice versa
X	Turns B and D on/off i.e. Black to white and vice versa
Y	Turns C and D on/off i.e. Black to white and vice versa
Z	Turns A and D on/off i.e. Black to white and vice versa

Answer

Q8. Which switch in the sequence is not working?

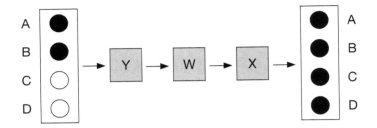

Switch	Function of the switch
W	Turns A and C on/off i.e. Black to white and vice versa
X	Turns B and D on/off i.e. Black to white and vice versa
Y	Turns C and D on/off i.e. Black to white and vice versa
Z	Turns A and D on/off i.e. Black to white and vice versa

Answer

Q9. Which switch in the sequence is not working?

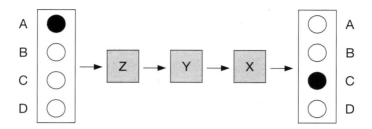

Switch	Function of the switch
W	Turns A and C on/off i.e. Black to white and vice versa
X	Turns B and D on/off i.e. Black to white and vice versa
Y	Turns C and D on/off i.e. Black to white and vice versa
Z	Turns A and D on/off i.e. Black to white and vice versa

Answer [   ]

Q10. Which switch in the sequence is not working?

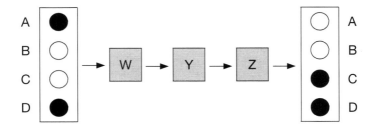

Switch	Function of the switch
W	Turns A and C on/off i.e. Black to white and vice versa
X	Turns B and D on/off i.e. Black to white and vice versa
Y	Turns C and D on/off i.e. Black to white and vice versa
Z	Turns A and D on/off i.e. Black to white and vice versa

Answer [   ]

ANSWERS TO CHECKING TESTS

1.   Switch X

2.   Switch W

3.   Switch X

4.   Switch Y

5.   Switch Z

6.   Switch Z

7.   Switch W

8.   Switch W

9.   Switch X

10. Switch Y

ASSESSING INFORMATION TESTS

This tests comprises of three areas, each designed to test your ability in regards to the rules and procedures of train companies.

ASSESSING INFORMATION PART 1

This part of the test assesses your aptitude to learn and recall job related information and to learn new procedures and regulations. At the assessment centre you will listen to some instructions being read aloud on an audio tape.

Whilst they are being read aloud you will also be given a printed copy of the instructions. You will then have the chance to study and learn the information. You can make notes on scrap paper provided, although both these and the printed copy of the instructions will be collected before you are asked to answer some questions. After studying the passage you will be asked to answer a number of multiple-choice questions based on the information contained within it.

For each question you will have four or five possible answers and you must select the one which is correct. I have now provided you with a sample test to give you an idea of what you will undertake during the real test. Please note, the passage in the following sample test is not be used during the real test.

TEST 1, SECTION 1

You have 4 minutes only to read the following passage and take notes before answering the questions on the following page.

Train tracks are made up of three main components: the metal rails, the sleepers that sit firmly underneath the rails and the ballast – the crushed rock segments that form a bed for the tracks to lie in.

A tamping machine, or a ballast tamper, is a machine that can be used for raising, straightening and altering the tracks. It is a machine that compresses the track ballast (the crushed segments of rock) under the rail track in order to make it more durable. Originally, this work was done manually, whereby labourers would use beaters as a way of pressing down the rock. Despite being faster, more accurate, efficient and less intensive, tamping machines are essential for the production and usage of creating stable tracks from concentre, typically weighing 250 kg.

For train tracks to work efficiently, the alignment of the tracks must be seamless. The sleepers that sit firmly underneath the rails, must also sit firmly in the crushed rock. If a track has been used for many years, or changes to the track have been made, the alignment of all three components needs to be altered in order to remain stable and effective. The gaps in the underlying rock bed need to be filled so that the sleepers do not move as a train passes along. This allows the train to run smoothly and ultimately reduces noise, vibrations and more importantly, any hazards.

Tamping machines can be used to fix these gaps by placing them on the track. It then conducts vibrations with hydraulic 'fingers' to remove all the gaps in the ballast, and align the

track up. These machines are very noisy and often cause disruption. Not only are the machines themselves noisy, but they also trigger track alarms which act as a warning sign for workers of approaching trains.

Most tamping jobs are conducted during the night, in order to avoid disrupting train services. By conducting this job at night, therefore can affect nearby neighbourhoods for one or two nights. Due to tamping machines being a part of regular maintenance work, Train Operating Companies are often unable to notify neighbourhoods that may be disturbed.

Question 1

Name **one** component that makes up the train tracks. Three **possible** answers.

Answer [   ]

Question 2

What is the name of the machine that is used in order to compress the crushed rock underneath the rail tracks?

A. Tampering machine

B. Tangent machine

C. Hydraulics machine

D. Tamping machine

E. Tramping machine

Answer [   ]

Question 3

What is the typical weight of the concrete used in the production process?

A. 150 kg

B. 200 kg

C. 250 kg

D. 300 kg

E. 350 kg

Answer [   ]

Question 4

The machine compresses the rock underneath the tracks, in order to make the tracks more....

A. Flexible

B. Diverse

C. Tangent

D. Resistant

E. Durable

Answer [   ]

Question 5

Whereabouts are the sleepers positioned?

A. Underneath the ballast

B. To the side of the ballast

C. Underneath the rails

D. To the side of the rails

E. On top of the rails

Answer [   ]

Question 6
What is the main job of the machine?

A. To compress the rock

B. To align the rails

C. To generate vibrations

D. To assist the trains mobility

E. To fix any gaps and voids in the track alignment

Answer

Question 7
What does these machines often trigger?

A. Signals

B. Mobility

C. Light

D. Alarms

E. Cannot be determined

Answer

Question 8
The alarms have been triggered. What is the reason for the alarm?

A. The sound of the job completed

B. To warn workers of an approaching train

C. The sound of the job beginning

D. The warn neighbours of work in progress

E. Cannot be determined

Answer [   ]

Question 9
What time, day or night, are tamping machines often used?

Answer [   ]

Question 10
What does this machinery conduct? **Two** answers needed.

A. Heat

B. Vibrations

C. Light

D. Noise

E. Mobility

Answer [   ]

Question 11
How was this job done originally?

Answer [   ]

Question 12
How often are the neighbourhoods living close by, notified of work with these machines?

A. Very often

B. Often

C. Neutral

D. Hardly ever

E. Never

Answer [   ]

Question 13
What is another name of the type of machine used?

Answer [   ]

Question 14

Why might the train track have gaps in the ballast?

  A. Animals digging holes underneath the train tracks

  B. The rock has eroded

  C. The tracks have been used for many years

  D. The infrastructure was not made correctly

  E. Cannot be determined

Answer

ANSWERS TO TEST 1, SECTION 1

Q1. Metal rails, the sleepers or the ballast – you are only asked for one answer, and so any of these answers will be correct.

Q2. D = tamping machine

Q3. C = 250 kg

Q4. E = durable

Q5. C = underneath the rails

Q6. E = to fix any gap or void in the track alignment

Q7. D = alarms

Q8. B = to warn workers of an approaching train

Q9. Night

Q10. B = vibrations and D = noise

Q11. Manually, with the use of beaters

Q12. D = hardly ever

Q13. Ballast tamper

Q14. C = has been used for many years

TEST 1, SECTION 2

You have 4 minutes only to read the following passage and take notes before answering the questions on the following page.

Freight trains are primarily used to transport cargo and goods, as opposed to transporting passengers. The railway network in Great Britain has been used to transport goods of various types and in various contingencies since the early 19th century. Whilst good traffic in the UK is considerably lower than other countries, it continues to be used, and continues to grow.

Rail freight has become extremely vital in regards to Britain's economic success. It is argued that using rail freight has contributed to over £800 million to the economy. Not only that, but it has also reduced congestion and carbon emissions, and therefore making this use of transportation more environmentally friendly.

Whether it is transporting raw materials for manufacturing purposes, fuels for electrical generations or consumer goods, businesses in the UK rely on freight trains to transport the cargo in an environmentally friendly and efficient way.

The UK has become more reliant on the use of rail freight which provides a faster, safer, greener and efficient way of transporting loads of cargo. It has been said that rail freight is expected to grow in demand by 30% in the next decade. This is equivalent to 240 additional freight trains per day.

In order to maintain and uphold this level of continual growth and demand for freight trains, train operating companies will work in partnership with the government to move cargo transports off of the road, and improve the quality of life by substantially reducing carbon emissions.

It is fact that, on average, a gallon of fuel will move a tonne of goods 246 miles on rail, but only 88 miles by road. Also, each freight train that is used, takes 60 HGV lorries off the road, ultimately helping carbon emissions.

During the First World War, it was renowned as the "Railway War". Thousands of tonnes of supplies and munitions were distributed all over Great Britain, whereby the supplies were dispatched from ports in the South East to be shipped over to France and the Front Line. A number of programmes were instigated in order for railways to meet the huge demands of the wartime. The Common User Agreement, conducted under the Coal Transport Act of 1917 are two examples of programmes that ultimately enabled better railway services. Over 100 train operating companies collaborated on these programmes and worked together in aid of national interest.

Question 1
What do freight trains carry?

A. Passengers

B. Cargo

C. Passengers and cargo

D. Cannot be determined

Answer [   ]

Question 2
How long has freight trains been in use in Great Britain?

A. Early 17th century

B. Late 17th century

C. Early 18th century

D. Late 18th century

E. Early 19th century

Answer [   ]

Question 3

The use of rail freight for Britain has been extremely vital in regards to…

A. Government success

B. Train Operating Companies becoming more popular

C. Economical success

D. Transport safety

E. Cannot be determined

Answer

Question 4

On average, how much has rail freight contributed to the economy?

A. £600 million

B. £800 million

C. £300 million

D. £500 million

E. £900 million

Answer

Question 5

Which two of the following answers can be concluded from rail freight being more environmentally friendly? **Two** answers required.

A. Reduces carbon emissions

B. Reduces the use of HGV's

C. Reduces cost

D. Reduces congestion

E. Reduces numerous transportation methods

Answer

Question 6

On average, a gallon of fuel for freight trains can move a tonne of goods how far?

A. 88 miles

B. 100 miles

C. 246 miles

D. 276 miles

E. 44 miles

Answer

Question 7
On average, a gallon of fuel for road usage can move a tonne of goods how far?

A. 246 miles

B. 44 miles

C. 102 miles

D. 88 miles

E. 70 miles

Answer

Question 8
If a freight train is used, how many HGV lorries are taken off the road?

A. 40

B. 60

C. 30

D. 70

E. 80

Answer

Question 9

How much are freight trains expected to grow in demand within one decade?

A. 20%

B. 70%

C. 50%

D. 40%

E. 30%

Answer ☐

Question 10

If freight trains continue to grow at the rate that is expected, how many additional freight trains will be used per day?

A. 210

B. 240

C. 200

D. 180

E. 190

Answer ☐

Question 11

How many train companies collaborated on the programmes that were instigated during the First World War?

A. Over 50

B. Over 60

C. Over 20

D. Over 80

E. Over 100

Answer

Question 12

What was the name of the Act that enabled better transport services during World War I?

A. Coal Transport Act 1921

B. Coal Transport Act 1917

C. Coal Transport Act 1912

D. Coal Transport Act 1931

E. Coal Transport Act 1940

Answer

Question 13

What was the First World War also known as?

A. Britain's War

B. British Railway War

C. Front Line War

D. Railway War

E. Cannot be determined

Answer [   ]

Question 14

Where were the supplies being shipped? **Two** answers required.

A. Germany

B. France

C. Front Line

D. England

E. Cannot be determined

Answer [   ]

ANSWERS TO TEST 1, SECTION 2

Q1. B = cargo

Q2. E = early 19th century

Q3. C = economical success

Q4. B = £800 million

Q5. A = reduces carbon emissions, D = reduces congestion

Q6. C = 246 miles

Q7. D = 88 miles

Q8. B = 60

Q9. E = 30%

Q10. B = 240

Q11. E = over 100

Q12. B = Coal Transport Act 1917

Q13. D = Railway War

Q14. B = France, C = Front Line

ASSESSING INFORMATION PART 2

This part of the trainability assessment measures your aptitude to apply rules to a series of diagrams. This test measures your ability to learn new rules and procedures. For the test on the assessment day you will be asked 20 questions. Each question has three or four diagrams with each diagram featuring one or more trains on a railway track. This track is divided into sections, with a signal between each section. The trains move from left to right, passing through signals onto the next section of the track.

These instructions will explain what the test is about, what you will be asked to do, and how to work out the answers to the questions. There are examples for you to follow and then some practice questions for you to try out before you start the test itself.

Here is an example of the type of diagram you will see in a question:

In each diagram there will be one signal that has a question mark above it.

This is the signal that you will be asked to look at, to judge whether it should be green (so that the train can pass through the signal) or red (so that the train will stay where it is). To do this you will look at some rules about the track which will be written down for you in the instructions. These rules are concerned with the safety aspect of controlling the movement of trains.

By using the key that follows to work out what each figure represents, you can see that there is a train waiting on the left hand side of the track. The question shows a train with 5 windows so therefore is has 5 carriages. The signal to its immediate right is red, which means that the train cannot move onto the next section of track. The section of track between the two signals is the length of 4 carriages, and the level crossing is down. This signal on the far right hand side of the diagram is green, which means that a train can pass through the signal onto the next section of track.

KEY TO QUESTION

Signals
     R   Signal is set at red, meaning STOP

     G   Signal is set at green, meaning GO

Track
     - - - - - - - -   Track is 4 carriages long

     ◇◇◇◇◇◇◇◇◇◇   Track is 5 carriages long

     • • • • • • • • • •   Track is 6 carriages long

     ————————   Track is 10 carriages long

Train
     Each window on the train represents one carriage

     ▮▮▮▮   This train has 4 carriages

     ▮▮▮▮▮   This train has 5 carriages

Signals
     Level crossing is down, so the road traffic is not moving across the railway track

     Level crossing is up, so the road traffic is moving across the railway track

When you have worked this out, look at the signal with the question mark over it, and use the rules in the key to assess whether it would be safe to change the signal to green, which would let the train move onto the next section of track.

Now that you have seen the type of diagram that will feature in the test, you need to know what the rules are that determine whether the train is allowed through the signal onto the next section of track.

The rules are as follows:

- The signal must be green before the train is allowed to pass through it.

- If the level crossing is open cars can drive across the track, therefore the train cannot be allowed to go through the signal onto this piece of track. This means that the signal should stay at red so that the train cannot move through the signal.

- There can only be one train sitting between two signals. If there is a train already sitting between two signals, and the signal to the right of it is red, then the signal to the left of it must also be red to prevent any other trains moving onto the same piece of track. However, if the signal to the right is green, this means that the train will be moving off, so another train could move onto the track; therefore the signal to the left can be green as it will be safe for another train to move onto the track.

Let's now take a look at another sample test question:

SAMPLE ASSESSING INFORMATION PART 2 TEST QUESTION

In the example the signal to the right of the middle section is red. This means that the train cannot move onto the next section of track. Therefore the signal with the question mark shows it should stay red so the 2 trains are not in the same section of track.

Now that you understand how the test works, try the 10 sample questions that follow. You have 10 minutes to complete the test.

SAMPLE ASSESSING INFORMATION PART 2 TEST QUESTION 1

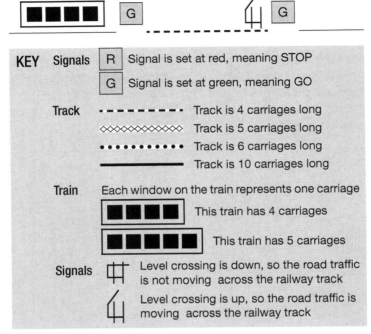

The rules are as follows:

- The signal must be green before the train is allowed to pass through it.
- If the level crossing is open cars can drive across the track, therefore the train cannot be allowed to go through the signal onto this piece of track. This means that the signal should stay at red so that the train cannot move through the signal.
- There can only be one train sitting between two signals. If there is a train already sitting between two signals, and the signal to the right of it is red, then the signal to the left of it must also be red to prevent any other trains moving onto the same piece of track. However, if the signal to the right is green, this means that the train will be moving off, so another train could move onto the track; therefore the signal to the left can be green as it will be safe for another train to move onto the track.

Answer [   ]

SAMPLE ASSESSING INFORMATION PART 2 TEST QUESTION 2

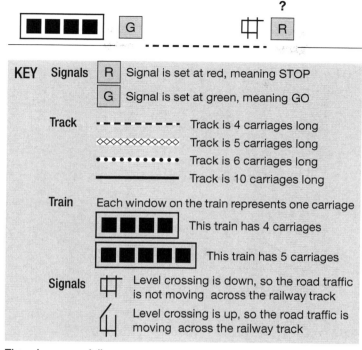

The rules are as follows:

- The signal must be green before the train is allowed to pass through it.

- If the level crossing is open cars can drive across the track, therefore the train cannot be allowed to go through the signal onto this piece of track. This means that the signal should stay at red so that the train cannot move through the signal.

- There can only be one train sitting between two signals. If there is a train already sitting between two signals, and the signal to the right of it is red, then the signal to the left of it must also be red to prevent any other trains moving onto the same piece of track. However, if the signal to the right is green, this means that the train will be moving off, so another train could move onto the track; therefore the signal to the left can be green as it will be safe for another train to move onto the track.

Answer [   ]

SAMPLE ASSESSING INFORMATION PART 2 TEST QUESTION 3

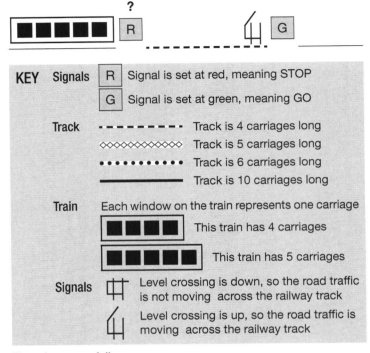

The rules are as follows:
- The signal must be green before the train is allowed to pass through it.
- If the level crossing is open cars can drive across the track, therefore the train cannot be allowed to go through the signal onto this piece of track. This means that the signal should stay at red so that the train cannot move through the signal.
- There can only be one train sitting between two signals. If there is a train already sitting between two signals, and the signal to the right of it is red, then the signal to the left of it must also be red to prevent any other trains moving onto the same piece of track. However, if the signal to the right is green, this means that the train will be moving off, so another train could move onto the track; therefore the signal to the left can be green as it will be safe for another train to move onto the track.

Answer [   ]

SAMPLE ASSESSING INFORMATION PART 2 TEST QUESTION 4

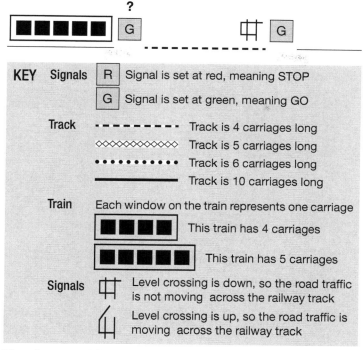

KEY Signals

R	Signal is set at red, meaning STOP
G	Signal is set at green, meaning GO

Track

- - - - - - - - Track is 4 carriages long
◇◇◇◇◇◇◇◇◇◇ Track is 5 carriages long
• • • • • • • • • • Track is 6 carriages long
———————— Track is 10 carriages long

Train Each window on the train represents one carriage

This train has 4 carriages

This train has 5 carriages

Signals Level crossing is down, so the road traffic is not moving across the railway track

Level crossing is up, so the road traffic is moving across the railway track

The rules are as follows:

- The signal must be green before the train is allowed to pass through it.
- If the level crossing is open cars can drive across the track, therefore the train cannot be allowed to go through the signal onto this piece of track. This means that the signal should stay at red so that the train cannot move through the signal.
- There can only be one train sitting between two signals. If there is a train already sitting between two signals, and the signal to the right of it is red, then the signal to the left of it must also be red to prevent any other trains moving onto the same piece of track. However, if the signal to the right is green, this means that the train will be moving off, so another train could move onto the track; therefore the signal to the left can be green as it will be safe for another train to move onto the track.

Answer [   ]

SAMPLE ASSESSING INFORMATION PART 2 TEST QUESTION 5

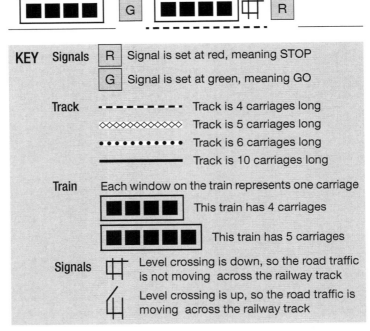

The rules are as follows:

- The signal must be green before the train is allowed to pass through it.
- If the level crossing is open cars can drive across the track, therefore the train cannot be allowed to go through the signal onto this piece of track. This means that the signal should stay at red so that the train cannot move through the signal.
- There can only be one train sitting between two signals. If there is a train already sitting between two signals, and the signal to the right of it is red, then the signal to the left of it must also be red to prevent any other trains moving onto the same piece of track. However, if the signal to the right is green, this means that the train will be moving off, so another train could move onto the track; therefore the signal to the left can be green as it will be safe for another train to move onto the track.

Answer

SAMPLE ASSESSING INFORMATION PART 2 TEST QUESTION 6

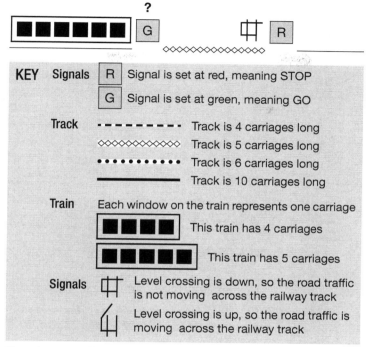

KEY

Signals

| R | Signal is set at red, meaning STOP |
| G | Signal is set at green, meaning GO |

Track

- - - - - - - - -   Track is 4 carriages long

◇◇◇◇◇◇◇◇◇◇◇   Track is 5 carriages long

• • • • • • • • • •   Track is 6 carriages long

————————   Track is 10 carriages long

Train   Each window on the train represents one carriage

This train has 4 carriages

This train has 5 carriages

Signals   Level crossing is down, so the road traffic is not moving across the railway track

Level crossing is up, so the road traffic is moving across the railway track

The rules are as follows:

- The signal must be green before the train is allowed to pass through it.
- If the level crossing is open cars can drive across the track, therefore the train cannot be allowed to go through the signal onto this piece of track. This means that the signal should stay at red so that the train cannot move through the signal.
- There can only be one train sitting between two signals. If there is a train already sitting between two signals, and the signal to the right of it is red, then the signal to the left of it must also be red to prevent any other trains moving onto the same piece of track. However, if the signal to the right is green, this means that the train will be moving off, so another train could move onto the track; therefore the signal to the left can be green as it will be safe for another train to move onto the track.

Answer

SAMPLE ASSESSING INFORMATION PART 2 TEST QUESTION 7

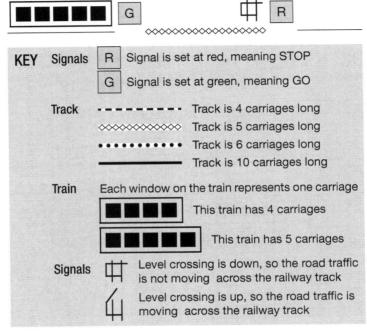

The rules are as follows:

- The signal must be green before the train is allowed to pass through it.

- If the level crossing is open cars can drive across the track, therefore the train cannot be allowed to go through the signal onto this piece of track. This means that the signal should stay at red so that the train cannot move through the signal.

- There can only be one train sitting between two signals. If there is a train already sitting between two signals, and the signal to the right of it is red, then the signal to the left of it must also be red to prevent any other trains moving onto the same piece of track. However, if the signal to the right is green, this means that the train will be moving off, so another train could move onto the track; therefore the signal to the left can be green as it will be safe for another train to move onto the track.

Answer

SAMPLE ASSESSING INFORMATION PART 2 TEST QUESTION 8

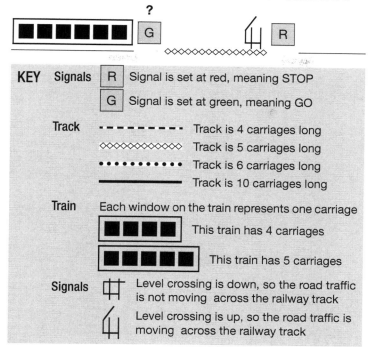

The rules are as follows:

- The signal must be green before the train is allowed to pass through it.

- If the level crossing is open cars can drive across the track, therefore the train cannot be allowed to go through the signal onto this piece of track. This means that the signal should stay at red so that the train cannot move through the signal.

- There can only be one train sitting between two signals. If there is a train already sitting between two signals, and the signal to the right of it is red, then the signal to the left of it must also be red to prevent any other trains moving onto the same piece of track. However, if the signal to the right is green, this means that the train will be moving off, so another train could move onto the track; therefore the signal to the left can be green as it will be safe for another train to move onto the track.

Answer

SAMPLE ASSESSING INFORMATION PART 2 TEST QUESTION 9

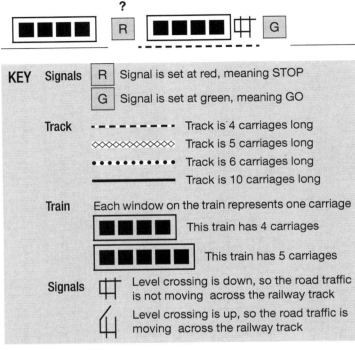

The rules are as follows:
- The signal must be green before the train is allowed to pass through it.
- If the level crossing is open cars can drive across the track, therefore the train cannot be allowed to go through the signal onto this piece of track. This means that the signal should stay at red so that the train cannot move through the signal.
- There can only be one train sitting between two signals. If there is a train already sitting between two signals, and the signal to the right of it is red, then the signal to the left of it must also be red to prevent any other trains moving onto the same piece of track. However, if the signal to the right is green, this means that the train will be moving off, so another train could move onto the track; therefore the signal to the left can be green as it will be safe for another train to move onto the track.

Answer

SAMPLE ASSESSING INFORMATION PART 2 TEST QUESTION 10

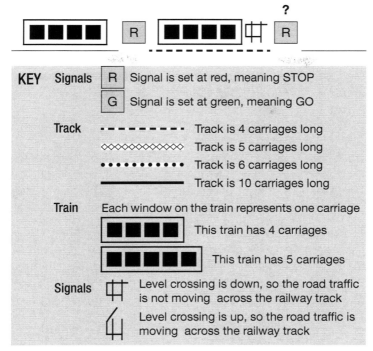

The rules are as follows:

- The signal must be green before the train is allowed to pass through it.

- If the level crossing is open cars can drive across the track, therefore the train cannot be allowed to go through the signal onto this piece of track. This means that the signal should stay at red so that the train cannot move through the signal.

- There can only be one train sitting between two signals. If there is a train already sitting between two signals, and the signal to the right of it is red, then the signal to the left of it must also be red to prevent any other trains moving onto the same piece of track. However, if the signal to the right is green, this means that the train will be moving off, so another train could move onto the track; therefore the signal to the left can be green as it will be safe for another train to move onto the track.

Answer

ANSWERS TO ASSESSING INFORMATION PART 2

1. The signal should stay red
Reason: If the level crossing is open cars can drive across the track, therefore the train cannot be allowed to go through the signal onto this piece of track. This means that the signal should stay at red so that the train cannot move through the signal.

2. The signal should change to green
Reason: The level crossing is closed to traffic and therefore, there is no reason why the train cannot continue on its journey. The track to the right of the red signal is 10 carriages long, which means there is sufficient track for the train to travel on.

3. The signal should stay red
Reason: If the level crossing is open cars can drive across the track, therefore the train cannot be allowed to go through the signal onto this piece of track. This means that the signal should stay at red so that the train cannot move through the signal.

4. The signal should change to green
Reason: The level crossing is down; therefore, there is no road traffic moving across the track. The train has 5 carriages so it is important that the signal to the right is also green, so that the train can continue on its journey.

5. The signal should change to red
Reason: There can only be one train sitting between two signals. If there is a train already sitting between two signals, and the signal to the right of it is red, then the signal to the left of it must also be red to prevent any other trains moving onto the same piece of track.

6. The signal should change to red

Reason: Although the level crossing is down and there is no road traffic moving across the track, the signal to the right is red and the track in the middle is only long enough for 5 carriages. Because the train to the left has 6 carriages, it will not fit on the middle section of the track.

7. The signal should change to green

Reason: The level crossing is down and there is no road traffic moving across the track. Although the signal to the right is red, the track in the middle is long enough for 5 carriages. Because the train to the left has 5 carriages, it will fit on the middle section of the track.

8. The signal should change to red

Reason: The level crossing is up which means there is road traffic moving across the track. The train also has 6 carriages and the track in the middle will only accommodate 5 carriages as per the key.

9. The signal should change to green

Reason: The level crossing is down which means there is no road traffic moving across the track. The train on the middle section can now move on to the final section of track as the signal to the right is also green.

10. The signal should change to green

Reason: The level crossing is down which means there is no road traffic moving across the track. The track on the right hand side is clear and therefore the train can now move off on its journey.

ASSESING INFORMATION PART 3

This part of the test measures your ability to work out train times and distances, based on the speed of different types of trains. The train types and speeds are shown below. Also shown is a diagram of a map which shows where the trains can go to.

Train type:	Speed:
Outer suburban	150 miles per hour
Rural	110 mph
Freight	85 mph
Light loco working	70 mph

There are four different types of train, each of which travels at a different speed, the lowest speed being 70 miles per hour and the highest being 150 miles per hour. Below are two examples of the types of questions you might be asked. Use your table and map to follow each question and the corresponding answer.

Example question 1

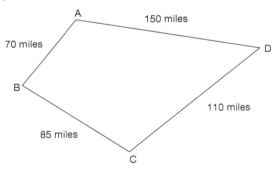

How long would it take an outer suburban train to travel from A to D?

Answer

One hour. This is because the distance between A and D is 150 miles and the outer suburban train travels 150 miles per hour, therefore it would take one hour for the train to travel between A and D.

Example question 2

If a rural train left D at 10:00, what time would it arrive at C?

Answer

11:00. This is because a rural train travels at 110 miles per hour and the distance between D and C is 110 miles, therefore the journey would take one hour. One hour from 10:00 is 11:00, so 11:00 is the answer.

For part 3 of the Assessing Information Test, you will be asked 20 questions in 15 minutes. Now move on to the sample speed and time test that follows. There are 20 questions and you have 15 minutes in which to complete them.

ASSESSING INFORMATION PART 3 EXERCISE

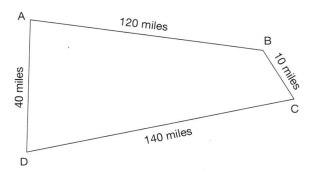

Train type	Speed
Outer suburban	120 miles per hour
Rural	80 mph
Freight	40 mph
Light loco working	70 mph

Q1. How long will it take a light loco working train to travel from C to D?

Answer

Q2. How long will it take a freight train to travel from A to B?

Answer

Q3. How long will it take an outer suburban train to travel from A to B?

Answer

ASSESSING INFORMATION PART 3 EXERCISE

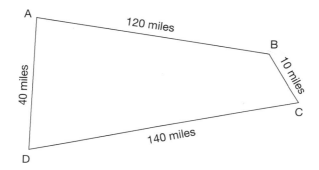

Train type	Speed
Outer suburban	120 miles per hour
Rural	80 mph
Freight	40 mph
Light loco working	70 mph

Q4. If a rural train left D at 9am, what time would it reach A?

Answer

Q5. If a light loco working train left C at 11pm, what time would it reach D?

Answer

Q6. If a rural train left D at 11.30am, what time would it reach B?

Answer

ASSESSING INFORMATION PART 3 EXERCISE

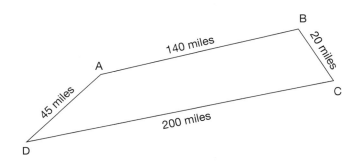

Train type	Speed
Outer suburban	150 miles per hour
Rural	90 mph
Freight	10 mph
Light loco working	70 mph

Q7. How long will it take a light loco working train to travel from A to B?

Answer [   ]

Q8. How long will it take a freight train to travel from A to C?

Answer [   ]

Q9. How long will it take an outer suburban train to travel from C to D?

Answer [   ]

ASSESSING INFORMATION PART 3 EXERCISE

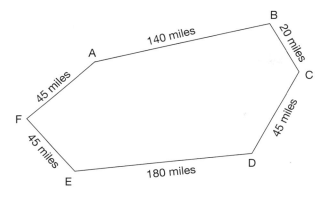

Train type	Speed
Outer suburban	120 miles per hour
Rural	90 mph
Freight	20 mph
Light loco working	70 mph

Q10. How long will it take an outer suburban train to travel from A to B?

Answer [   ]

Q11. How long will it take a freight train to travel from A to C?

Answer [   ]

Q12. How long will it take a rural train to travel from C to F?

Answer [   ]

ASSESSING INFORMATION PART 3 EXERCISE

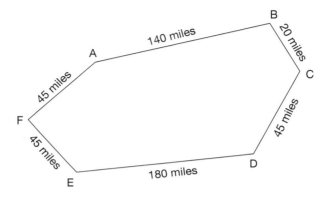

Train type	Speed
Outer suburban	120 miles per hour
Rural	90 mph
Freight	20 mph
Light loco working	70 mph

Q13. If a freight train left A at 9am, what time would it reach C?

Answer

Q14. If a rural train left E at 8.45pm, what time would it reach A?

Answer

Q15. If an out suburban train left A at 7am, what time would it reach C?

Answer

ASSESSING INFORMATION PART 3 EXERCISE

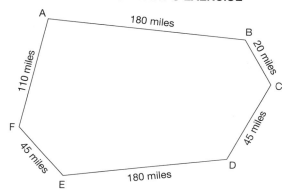

Train type	Speed
Outer suburban	120 miles per hour
Rural	70 mph
Freight	5 mph
Light loco working	90 mph

Q16. How long will it take an outer suburban train to travel from A to C?

Answer

Q17. How long will it take a freight train to travel from F to C?

Answer

Q18. How long will it take an outer suburban train to travel from A to F?

Answer

ASSESSING INFORMATION PART 3 EXERCISE

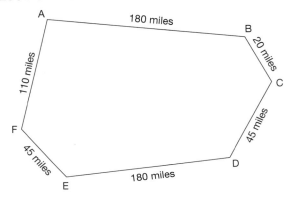

Train type	Speed
Outer suburban	120 miles per hour
Rural	70 mph
Freight	5 mph
Light loco working	90 mph

Q19. If a freight train left F at 9am, what time would it reach A?

Answer [   ]

Q20. If a light loco train left C at 6.45am, what time would it reach F?

Answer [   ]

Now check your answers before moving on to the next section of the guide

ANSWERS TO ASSESSING INFORMATION PART 3

Q1. 2 hours

Q2. 3 hours

Q3. 1 hour

Q4. 9.30am

Q5. 1am

Q6. 1.30pm

Q7. 2 hours

Q8. 16 hours

Q9. 1 hour 20 minutes

Q10. 1 hour 10 minutes

Q11. 8 hours

Q12. 3 hours

Q13. 5pm

Q14. 9.45pm

Q15. 8.20am

Q16. 1 hour 40 minutes

Q17. 62 hours

Q18. 3 hours and 50 minutes

Q19. 7am

Q20. 9.45am

CHAPTER SIX
THE INTERVIEW

During this section of the guide I will provide you with some useful tips on how to prepare for the Railway Signaller interview. The interview does not have to be a daunting process, providing that is, you prepare effectively. Yes, any interview can be a nerve-wracking experience, but if you prepare in the right areas this will give the confidence you need to pass with flying colours. Within this section of the guide I have provided you with a number of sample questions that you may get asked during your interview. The structured interview may be carried out on the same day as the assessment centre, so make sure you have prepared for it well in advance.

HOW TO PREPARE EFFECTIVELY

During your preparation for the interview I would recommend that you concentrate on the following three key areas:

- Interview technique;

- Research;

- Responding to the interview questions.

Each of the above areas are equally important. I will now go into each one of them in detail:

INTERVIEW TECHNIQUE

Interview technique covers a number of different areas. The majority of candidates will pay it little, if any attention at all. Interview technique basically involves the following key areas:

- **Creating the right impression.** When you walk into the interview room you should stand up tall, smile and be polite and courteous to the panel. Do not sit down in the interview chair until invited to do so.

- **Being presentable.** During my time as an interviewer for a number of different jobs I have been amazed at the number of people who turn up inappropriately dressed. I have seen people turn up for interviews in jeans, t shirts and trainers! I strongly advise that you take the time to look smart and presentable. Remember you are applying to join an organisation that may require you to wear a uniform. If you dress smart and formal for the interview then you are far more likely to wear your uniform with pride.

- **Sitting in the chair.** The interview could last for up to an hour, depending on the length of your responses to the questions. This is a long time to concentrate for. Whilst in the interview chair sit up right at all times and never slouch.

- **Motivation.** Throughout the duration of the interview demonstrate a high level of motivation and enthusiasm.

You do not want to come across as desperate, but conversely you must come across as highly motivated and determined to be successful. Always smile and be respectful of the interview panel.

- **Communication.** When communicating with the interview panel look them in the eye. This shows a level of confidence. You should also communicate in a clear and concise manner where possible. Remember that one of the key requirements for the role of a Railway Signaller is that of effective communication.

- **Asking questions.** At the end of the interview you will be given the opportunity to ask questions. This is where some candidates let themselves down with silly or inappropriate questions that relate to leave or sick pay. It is quite acceptable to ask a couple of questions, however, keep them simple and relevant. Examples of good questions to ask are:

    Q. If I am successful, how long would it be before I start my training course as a Railway Signaller?

    Q. I have been looking into your company and I have been impressed with the 'new lines programme' that helps to keep passengers informed. Has this been successful and well-received?

    Q. Whilst I wait to hear whether or not I am successful, is there any additional literature or information I could study and read about the train operating company to further my knowledge?

- **A final parting statement.** Once the interview has finished and you have asked your questions, you may wish to finish off with a final statement. Your final statement should say something about your desire and

passion for becoming a Railway Signaller. The following is a good example of a final statement:

"I would like to say thank you for giving me the opportunity to be interviewed for the post today. Over the last few months I have been working hard to learn about the role and also about Network Rail. If I am successful then I promise you that I will be a loyal, safety-conscious and professional member of your team. Thank you."

RESEARCH

As you can imagine, in the build-up to the interview you will need to carry out plenty of research. Research, that is, in relation to the role of a Signaller and also the organisation that you are applying to join. Here is a list of the more important areas I recommend that you study:

- The job description and person specification for the job that you are applying for.

- Your application form and the responses that you provided to all of the questions. You should also revisit your CV prior to the interview.

- The website of the organisation you are applying to join. What is their customer service charter? Do they have a mission statement? What services do they provide? What is their geographical area? How many people work for them? Who is the person in charge? What improvements are they currently making within the rail industry? What trains do they operate? Do they operate any schemes in order to improve customer service? What are the future plans of the company?

- Try to visit a train station or signal box that comes under the jurisdiction of Network Rail. Speak to some of the

staff at the station and ask them questions about the role they perform. Try to find out as much as possible about the organisation as this will shine through during the interview. If you get the opportunity, speak to a qualified Railway Signallers who work for Network Rail. You may also decide to telephone Network Rail's Human Resources department and ask if you can go along to find out a little bit more about their organisation and what they expect from their employees.

RESPONDING TO THE INTERVIEW QUESTIONS

If I were preparing for the interview right now, I would take each area of the role individually and prepare a detailed response setting out where I meet the requirements of it.

Your response to each question that relates to the role must be 'specific' in nature. This means that you need to provide an example of where you have already demonstrated the skills that are required under the job description or person specification in a previous role or situation. Do not fall into the trap of providing a 'generic' response that details what you 'would do' if the situation arose. Try to structure your responses in a logical and concise manner. The way to achieve this is to use the 'STAR' method of interview question response construction:

Situation
Start off your response to the interview question by explaining what the 'situation' was and who was involved.

Task
Once you have detailed the situation, explain what the 'task' was, or what needed to be done.

Action

Now explain what 'action' you took, and what action others took. Also explain why you took this particular course of action.

Result

Now explain what the outcome or result was following your actions and those of others. Try to demonstrate in your response that the result was positive because of the action you took.

Finally, explain to the panel what you would do differently if the same situation arose again. It is good to be reflective at the end of your responses. This demonstrates a level of maturity and it will also show the panel that you are willing to learn from every experience.

THE DIFFERENT TYPES OF INTERVIEW QUESTIONS

Basically there are two different types of interview questions that you could be asked. I will try to explain each of them and what they mean:

1. **Generic questions about you and your knowledge of the organisation and the Railway Signaller's role.**

Generic questions can be in any format. There is no particular structure to this type of question but they are generally far easier to respond to. Examples of generic questions would include:

- Why do you want to become a Railway Signaller?

- What has attracted you to this organisation in particular?

- What have you learnt about the role?

- Why should we choose you against the other applicants?

2. Role related questions.

This type of question is more common during the structured interview and includes questions that are based around the job description/person specification. Examples of role related questions include:

- Being able to work under pressure.

- Following rules or guidelines.

- Providing a high level of customer service.

- Working as part of a team to achieve a task.

- Communicating a message to an individual or a group of people.

- Working with people from different backgrounds.

- Being flexible in a work-related situation.

- Working unsociable hours.

- Making quick and timely decisions under stress.

On the following pages I have provided you with a number of sample interview questions and responses to assist you in your preparation. Please remember that the responses provided are not to be copied under any circumstances. Use them as a basis for your preparation taking examples from your own individual experiences and knowledge.

SAMPLE INTERVIEW QUESTIONS AND RESPONSES

QUESTION 1

Why do you want to become a Signaller?

This question is inevitable, so it is important that you ensure you have a suitable answer prepared. Many people will respond with a standard answer such as "It's something that I've always wanted do since I was young". Whilst this is OK you need to back it up with genuine reasons that relate to the organisation you are applying for and other important reasons, such as a desire to learn new skills and a desire to work in an environment that requires a calm disposition during pressurised situations.

This type of question may be posed in a number of different formats such as the following:

Q. Why do you want to become a Signaller with our Company?

Q. What has attracted you to the role?

Now take a look at the following sample response which will help you to prepare for this type of question. Once you have read it, use the template on the next page to create your own response based upon your own experiences and knowledge.

SAMPLE RESPONSE

Why do you want to become a Signaller?

"I have wanted to become a Signaller for many years now and have been preparing for the role for a long time. I have been researching Network Rail in the build-up to submitting my application and I have been impressed with the way your company operates. It sets itself high standards in terms of the service it provides and the safety standards that are expected of its employees.

Apart from the fact that being a Rail Signaller is quite a varied and responsible job, I also very much enjoy new and different challenges. I understand that as a Signaller there are a lot of new skills to learn, especially during the early years. The type of person I am means that I would work hard to ensure that I passed every exam or assessment first time. I also enjoy working in an environment where a high level of service is essential and an ability to make important decisions whilst under pressure.

As a Signaller you are responsible for the safety of the passengers, rolling stock and train drivers, and I would enjoy the high level of responsibility that comes with the position."

TEMPLATE FOR QUESTION 1

Why do you want to become a Signaller?

QUESTION 2

Why do you want to work for our company?

Once again this is a question that is likely to come up during your interview. In order to prepare for this question you need to carry out some research about Network Rail, or the organisation you are applying for, if it is not Network Rail. The best place to get this information is via their website. See the Useful Contacts section for a list of current Train Operating Companies and the Network Rail website.

When responding to this type of question, try to focus on the positive aspects of the company's work. Do they run any customer-focused initiatives or have they won any awards for quality of work or service? It is always good to make reference to the positive aspects of their work, but do not make mention of any current or previous bad press. I have now provided a sample response to this question to help you prepare. Once you have read it, take the time to construct your own answer using the template provided.

SAMPLE RESPONSE

Why do you want to work for our company?

"I have been carrying out a lot of research into your company in the build-up to the interview and I have been very impressed with the level of service you offer. In particular, I was impressed at the way you make it very easy for passengers or members of the public to provide feedback, in particular on issues such as animals and wildlife, noise from trains form, work from engineers and staff, railway equipment and fencing issues. I also understand that, in order to meet future demand on a whole network basis, you develop and implement a Long Term Planning Process which builds on the success of your Route Utilisation Strategy programme. Network Rail is clearly a forward-thinking organisation and I feel that I would have excellent career opportunities if I was successful and therefore be very happy in my role as a Signaller."

TEMPLATE FOR QUESTION 2

Why do you want to work for our company?

QUESTION 3

What can you tell us about the role of a Signaller?

You must be well-prepared for this question prior to your interview. If you don't know what the role involves, then you shouldn't be applying for the post. When responding to this question, make sure you make reference to the job/person specification for the role. The job specification is a 'blueprint' for the role that you will be required to perform whilst working as a Railway Signaller. Therefore, it is essential that you know it. An example of a Railway Signaller's duties/person specification is detailed below:

Example Railway Signaller Job Description

Your decisions make all the difference. Taking the lead on signalling during your shift, you'll take great care to make sure trains travel safely and efficiently along the network. You'll keep Britain moving.

About the role
As a guardian of safety and good communications on the railway, you'll ensure the safe passage of trains. Maintaining the highest standards in every action you take, you'll make sure each decision is thought through, following clear, calm and methodical analysis. Even under pressure, your standards will never slip.

You'll work on a shift basis. As the focal point of railway operations in your assigned area, you'll be expected to take the lead in your duties during your shift. That means you'll take command of situations, with an assertive approach and clear communication.

If you pass our assessment, you'll be required to undertake a 9-week residential course at a state-of-the-art training centre. This will be followed by further training within your appointed signal box. We'll make sure you have all the knowledge and skills you need to succeed.

To join us, you'll need to demonstrate:

- The ability to concentrate for long periods

- A calm, methodical and precise approach to your work

- Excellent communication skills

- Good hearing and eyesight, with normal colour perception

- Your own transport, so you can reach your base day and night

We'll expect you to be:

- Able to assess situations and consider the impact of your decisions

- Highly conscientious

- Willing and able to work shifts, including evenings and weekends

Now take a look at the sample response before constructing your own response using the template provided.

SAMPLE RESPONSE

What can you tell us about the role of a Railway Signaller?

"I understand that the role involves a high level of responsibility, concentration flexibility and good communication skills. To begin with, Signallers are guardians of safety and need to be able to provide accurate and timely communications on the railway to ensure the safe passage of trains. Signallers must also maintain the highest standards in every action they take, making sure each decision is thought through clearly, calmly and methodically. Inevitably, Railway Signallers will be required to work under pressure, and therefore, their standards must never slip.

In addition to this they must work on a shift basis and also unsociable hours. Signallers are the focal point of railway operations and I would be expected to take the lead in my duties during the shift. That means I will take command of situations, with an assertive approach and clear communication."

TEMPLATE FOR QUESTION 3

What can you tell us about the role of a Railway Signaller?

QUESTION 4

What skills do you possess that you think would be an asset to our team?

When responding to questions of this nature, try to match your skills with the skills that are required of a Railway Signaller. On the Network Rail website, you should be able to see the type of person they are looking to employ. This will normally be located in the recruitment section.

An example of this would be:

"Our signallers operate the signals and points that help make sure trains run safely and on time. You'll be a guardian for safety and will be responsible for maintaining safety standards not just when the railway is running normally but also when there is disruption. This calls for excellent communications, a strong sense of responsibility, an ability to work under pressure and the ability to make systematic decisions in a timely fashion."

Just by looking at the Network Rail website, you should be able to obtain some clues as to the type of person they are seeking to employ. Try to think of the skills that are required to perform the role you are applying for and include them in your response. The following is a sample response to the question. Once you have read it, take the time to construct your own response using the template provided.

SAMPLE RESPONSE

What skills do you possess that you think would be an asset to our team?

"I am a very conscientious person who takes the time to learn and develop new skills correctly. I have vast experience working in a customer-focused/service-related environment and fully understand that delivering outstanding service is important. Without the passenger there would be no company, so it is important that every member of the team works towards providing a high level of service.

I believe I have the skills, knowledge and experience to do this. I am a very good team player and can always be relied upon to carry out my role to the highest of standards. I am a flexible person and understand that there is a need to be available at short notice to cover duties if required. In addition to these skills and attributes, I am an excellent communicator. I have experience of having to communicate to customers in my previous role and believe that this would be an asset in the role of a Railway signaller. I am also fully aware of the importance of being able to communicate information accurately and timely.

I am highly safety-conscious and have a health and safety qualification to my name. Therefore, I can be relied upon to perform all procedures relevant to the codes of conduct and will not put myself or others in any danger whatsoever. Finally, I am very good at learning new skills which means that I will work hard to pass all of my exams if I am successful in becoming a trainee Railway Signaller."

TEMPLATE FOR QUESTION 4

What skills do you possess that you think would be an asset to our team?

QUESTION 5

Can you tell us about a situation when you have had to work under pressure?

The role of a Railway Signaller will sometimes involve a requirement to work under pressure. Therefore, the recruitment staff will want to know that you have the ability to perform in such an environment. If you have experience of working under pressure then you are far more likely to succeed in the role. When responding to a question of this nature, try to provide an actual example of where you have achieved a task whilst being under pressure. Questions of this nature are sometimes included in the application form, so try to use a different example for the interview. I have provided you with a sample response to this question. Once you have read it, take the time to construct your own response based on your own individual experiences and knowledge using the template provided.

SAMPLE RESPONSE

Can you tell us about a situation when you have had to work under pressure?

"Yes, I can. In my current job as a car mechanic for a well-known company, I was presented with a difficult and pressurised situation. A member of the team had made a mistake and had fitted a number of wrong components to a car. The car in question was due to be picked up at 2pm and the customer had stated how important it was that his car was ready on time because he had an important meeting to attend. We only had two hours in which to resolve the issue and I volunteered to be the one who would carry out the work on the car. The problem was that we had three other customers in the workshop waiting for their cars too, so I was the only person who could be spared at that particular time. I worked solidly for the next two hours making sure that I meticulously carried out each task in line with our operating procedures. Even though I didn't finish the car until 2.10pm, I managed to achieve a very difficult task under pressurised conditions whilst keeping strictly to procedures and regulations."

TEMPLATE FOR QUESTION 5

Can you tell us about a situation when you have had to work under pressure?

QUESTION 6

Can you tell me about a time when you have worked as part of a team to achieve a goal?

Having the ability to work as part of a team is very important to the role of a Railway Signaller. Network Rail and the Train Operating Companies employ many people in different roles from Train Drivers to platform staff and from ticket office staff to cleaners. In fact, it is not uncommon for thousands of people to work for one particular TOC or company. Therefore, it is essential that every member of the team works together in order to achieve the ultimate goal of providing a high quality rail service. The recruitment staff will want to be certain that you can work effectively as part of a team, which is why you may be asked questions that relate to your team working experience.

There now follows a sample response to this question. Once you have read it, take time to construct your own response using the template provided.

SAMPLE RESPONSE

Can you tell me about a time when you have worked as part of a team to achieve a goal?

"Yes, I can. I like to keep fit and healthy and as part of this aim I play football for a local Sunday team. We had worked very hard to get to the cup final and we were faced with playing a very good opposition team who had recently won the league title. After only ten minutes of play, one of our players was sent off and we conceded a penalty as a result. Being one goal down and 80 minutes left to play we were faced with a mountain to climb. However, we all remembered our training and worked very hard in order to prevent any more goals being scored. Due to playing with ten players, I had to switch positions and play as a defender, something that I am not used to. The team worked brilliantly to hold off any further opposing goals and after 60 minutes we managed to get an equaliser. The game went to penalties in the end and we managed to win the cup. I believe I am an excellent team player and can always be relied upon to work as an effective team member at all times. I understand that being an effective team member is very important if Network Rail is to provide a high level of service to the passenger and the Train operating Companies it serves. However, above all of this, effective teamwork is essential in order to maintain the high safety standards that are set."

TEMPLATE FOR QUESTION 6

Can you tell me about a time when you have worked as part of a team to achieve a goal?

QUESTION 7

Can you provide us with an example of a project you have had to complete and the obstacles you had to overcome?

Having the ability to complete tasks and projects successfully demonstrates that you have the ability to complete your initial training course. Many people give up on things in life and fail to achieve their goals. The recruitment staff will need to be convinced that you are going to complete all training successfully and, if you can provide evidence of where you have already done this, then this will go in your favour. When responding to this type of question, try to think of a difficult, drawn out task that you achieved despite a number of obstacles that were in your way. You may choose to use examples from your work life or even from some recent academic work that you have carried out. Take a look at the following sample question before using the template provided to construct your own response based on your own experiences.

SAMPLE RESPONSE

Can you provide us with an example of a project you have had to complete and the obstacles you had to overcome?

"Yes I can. I recently successfully completed a NEBOSH course (National Examination Board in Occupational Safety and Health) via distance learning. The course took two years to complete in total and I had to carry out all studying in my own time whilst holding down my current job.

The biggest obstacle I had to overcome was finding the time to complete the work to the high standard that I wanted to achieve. I decided to manage my time effectively and I allocated two hours every evening of the working week in which to complete the work required. I found the time management difficult but I stuck with it and I was determined to complete the course. In the end I achieved very good results and I very much enjoyed the experience and challenge. I have a determined nature and I have the ability to concentrate for long periods of time when required. I can be relied upon to finish projects to a high standard."

TEMPLATE FOR QUESTION 7

Can you provide us with an example of a project you have had to complete and the obstacles you had to overcome?

QUESTION 8

Can you provide us with an example of a safety-related task that you have had to perform?

Safety is an extremely important part of the Railway Signallers role and the recruitment staff need to know that you are capable of working safely at all times. The term 'safety' should be an integral part of some of your responses during the interview. Making reference to the fact that you are aware of the importance of safety at every opportunity is a positive thing. When responding to safety-related questions try to include examples where you have had to work to, or follow, safety guidelines or procedures. If you have a safety qualification then it is definitely worthwhile mentioning this during your interview. Any relevant safety experience or related role should also be discussed.

Now take a look at the following sample response before using the template provided to construct your own response.

SAMPLE RESPONSE

Can you provide us with an example of a safety-related task that you have had to perform?

"I currently work as a gas fitter and I am often required to perform safety-related tasks. An example of one of these tasks would involve the installation of gas-fired boilers. When fitting a gas boiler I have to ensure that I carry out a number of safety checks during the installation stage which ensures my work is safe and to a high standard. I have been trained, and I am qualified, to carry out my work in accordance with strict safety guidelines. I also have a number of safety certificates to demonstrate my competence.

I am fully aware that if I do not carry out my job in accordance with safety guidelines there is the possibility that somebody may become injured or even killed."

TEMPLATE FOR QUESTION 8

Can you provide us with an example of a safety-related task that you have had to perform?

Hopefully you are now starting to get a feel for how you need to respond to the interview questions. The following set of interview questions are further examples of questions you could get asked during the interviews.

QUESTION 9

How do you think you would cope with working on your own and unsupervised for long periods?

Lone working can be an unfortunate part of the Railway Signallers job. You may spend many hours on your own and this can be a problem for many people. Even though you will be speaking to other members of your team, you will still be required to work unsupervised on occasions. You need to think carefully about this downside to the job. Can you cope with it? Do you have any experience of working on your own? If you do not then you will have to convince the panel that you can cope with it.

QUESTION 10

What is your sickness record like and what do you think is an acceptable level of sickness?

Most employers detest sickness and they especially detest sickness that is not genuine. For every day that an employee is off sick will cost Network Rail dearly. Therefore, they want to employ people who have a good sickness record. Obviously you cannot lie when responding to this question as the organisation you are applying for will carry out checks. The latter part of the question is simple to answer. Basically no amount of sickness is acceptable but sometimes genuine sickness cannot be helped. Remember to tell them that you

do not take time off sick unless absolutely necessary and you can be relied upon to come to work.

QUESTION 11

Have you ever worked during the night and how do you feel about working shifts?

Railway Signallers work irregular shifts and they will want to know that you can handle them. Speak to any person who works shifts and they will tell you that after a number of years they can start to take their toll. Remember to tell the panel that you are looking forward to working shifts and in particular night duties. If you can provide examples of where you have worked irregular shift patterns then remember to tell them.

QUESTION 12

Would you get bored of doing the same job, day in, day out?

Of course, the only answer here is no! It is essential that you can maintain concentration for long periods of time in this role.

QUESTION 13

How many people work for this organisation?

Questions that relate to facts and figures about the organisation might come up. They want to know that you are serious about joining them and that you are not just there to become a Railway Signaller. Make sure you study their website and find out as much about them as possible.

QUESTION 14

How do we measure performance with regards to train punctuality?

Once again, this is a question that relates to your knowledge of the organisation you are applying for. This kind of information can usually be found by visiting their website. The Public Performance Measure (PPM) is used by Network Rail as a tool to measure the percentage of trains which arrive at their destination on time. PPM combines figures for punctuality and reliability into a single performance measure. It is the industry standard measurement of performance. Nationally around 60% of delays to train services are attributed to Network Rail. As well as infrastructure faults, this figure includes external factors such as weather, trespass, vandalism, cable theft etc. These external factors account for approximately one third of the delays attributed to Network Rail and 20% of all national delays.

QUESTION 15

What are the mission and aims of this company?

Many organisations, including Network Rail and Train Operating Companies, set themselves aims and objectives. They usually relate to the high level of service that they promise to deliver. When you apply to become a Railway Signaller you should not only prepare for each stage of the selection process but you should also learn as much as possible about the company you are applying to join. Learning this kind of information is important and it will demonstrate your seriousness about joining their particular company.

QUESTION 16

Can you provide us with an example of when you have had to work in an emergency?

This question is also likely to be asked during the application form stage of the process. Being able to remain calm under pressure is very important and will form an integral part of your training. Maybe you have had to deal with an emergency at work or even in the home? Whatever example you decide to use, make sure you tell them that you stayed calm and focused on the task in hand. Make reference to the importance of safety during your response.

FINAL TIPS FOR PREPARING FOR THE INTERVIEW

- Make sure you turn up to your interview on time! Find out the route to the interview location well in advance and make sure you don't get stuck in traffic or have any problems parking. Prepare for these eventualities well in advance.

- Wear formal clothing for your interview. Make sure you are clean-shaven and your shoes are clean and polished. Remember that you will be representing the company if you are successful and your appearance is very important.

- Visit the website of the organisation you are applying for and learn information about how they operate and what they are about. This is important so that you can create an image that you are serious about working for them and not just interested in becoming a Railway Signaller.

- During your preparation for the interview, try to think of some recent examples of situations you have been in that are relevant to the role.

- When responding to the questions try to concentrate on what you have achieved so far during your life. It is important that you can demonstrate a track record of achievement.

- Make sure you smile during your interview. Sit up straight in the chair and do not fidget.

CHAPTER SEVEN
USEFUL CONTACTS

Within this section of the guide I have provided you with a list of Train Operating Companies and other useful websites that exist in England, Scotland and Wales.

Network Rail
www.networkrail.co.uk

Arriva Trains Wales
www.arrivatrainswales.co.uk
Arriva Trains Wales
St Mary's House
47 Penarth Road
Cardiff CF10 5DJ
0845 6061 660
customer.relations@arrivatrainswales.co.uk

C2C

www.c2c-online.co.uk
10th Floor,
207 Old Street,
London EC1V 9NR
0845 6014873
c2c.customerrelations@nationalexpress.com

Chiltern Railways

www.chilternrailways.co.uk
Chiltern Railways 2nd floor,
Western House
Rickfords Hill
Aylesbury
Buckinghamshire HP20 2RX
08456 005 165

CrossCountry

www.crosscountrytrains.co.uk
CrossCountry
Cannon House
18 The Priory
Queensway
Birmingham B4 6BS
0870 010 0084
info@crosscountrytrains.co.uk

East Coast

www.eastcoast.co.uk
East Coast House
25 Skeldergate House
York Y01 6DH
08457 225 225

East Midlands Trains

www.eastmidlandstrains.co.uk
1 Prospect Place
Millennium Way
Pride Park
Derby DE24 8HG
08457 125 678
getintouch@eastmidlandstrains.co.uk

Eurostar

www.eurostar.com
Times House
Bravingtons Walk
Regent Quarter
London N1 9AW
08701 606 600

First Capital Connect

www.firstcapitalconnect.co.uk

First Great Western

www.firstgreatwestern.co.uk
Head Office
Milford House
1 Milford Street
Swindon SN1 1HL
08457 000 125

First Hull Trains

www.hulltrains.co.uk
First Hull Trains
FREEPOST
RLYY-XSTG-YXCK
4th Floor

Europa House
184 Ferensway
HULL HU1 3UT
08456 769 905

First TransPennine Express
www.tpexpress.co.uk
Floor 7
Bridgewater House
60 Whitworth Street
Manchester M1 6LT
0845 600 1671

Gatwick Express
www.gatwickexpress.com
Go Ahead House
26-28 Addiscombe Road
Croydon CR9 5GA
0845 850 15 30

Grand Central
www.grandcentralrail.co.uk
River House
17 Museum Street
York YO1 7DJ
0845 6034852
info@grandcentralrail.com

Heathrow Connect
www.heathrowconnect.com

Heathrow Express
www.heathrowexpress.com
6th Floor

50 Eastbourne Terrace
Paddington
London W2 6LX
020 8750 6600

Island Line Trains
www.southwesttrains.co.uk
Ryde St Johns Road Station,
Ryde, Isle of Wight PO33 2BA
01983 812 591

London Midland
www.londonmidland.com
102 New Street
Birmingham B2 4JB
0121 634 2040
comments@londonmidland.com

London Overground
www.tfl.gov.uk/overground
London Overground Rail Operations
125 Finchley Road
London NW3 6HY
0845 601 4867

London Underground
www.tfl.gov.uk

Merseyrail
www.merseyrail.org
Rail House
Lord Nelson Street
Liverpool L1 1JF
0151 702 2534

National Express East Anglia
www.nationalexpresseastanglia.com
Floor One
Oliver's Yard
55 City Road
London EC1Y 1HQ
0845 600 7245
nxea.customerrelations@nationalexpress.com

Northern Rail
www.northernrail.org
Northern Rail Ltd
Northern House
9 Rougier Street
York YO1 6HZ
0845 00 00 125
customer.relations@northernrail.org

ScotRail
www.scotrail.co.uk
Atrium Court
50 Waterloo Street
Glasgow G2 6HQ
08700 005151

South West Trains
www.southwesttrains.co.uk
South West Trains
Friars Bridge Court
41-45 Blackfriars Road
London SE1 8NZ
08700 00 5151

Southeastern
www.southeasternrailway.co.uk
PO Box 63428
London SE1P 5FD
0845 000 2222

Stansted Express
www.stanstedexpress.com

Virgin Trains
www.virgintrains.co.uk
Virgin Trains
85 Smallbrook
Queensway
Birmingham B5 4HA
0845 000 8000

Wrexham & Shropshire
www.wrexhamandshropshire.co.uk
The Pump House
Coton Hill
Shrewsbury SY1 2DP
0845 260 5233
info@wrexhamandshropshire.co.uk

OTHER USEFUL WEBSITES

Rail Safety & Standards Board
www.rssb.co.uk

The Department for Transport
www.dft.gov.uk

Rail Technical Pages
www.railway-technical.com

how2become

Visit www.**how2become.co.uk**
to find more titles and courses that
will help you to pass the Railway
Signaller selection process, including:

- How to pass job interview books and DVD's.
- Railway Signaller tests.
- Train Driving books, DVDs and courses.
- Psychometric testing books and CD's.

www.how2become.com